The Unque Fire

C000132050

John G Greenshields,

with illustrations by Nyomi Lee Purves

Copyright © 2023 John G Greenshields and Nyomi
Lee Purves

All rights reserved.

ISBN: 9798391198390

DEDICATION

To all who have shared in my own journey with Jesus, and most of all to my beloved wife Rosemary, this book is dedicated.

May the Holy Spirit, who came at Pentecost with heavenly fire, visit us all afresh with the cleansing, purifying, enabling power of God.

INTRODUCTION

"What's next?" A question asked by a number of people, in the wake of my two devotional guides covering Luke's gospel. *The Rising Sun* offered a guide through Advent, focussing on chapters 1-2. *Following Jesus,* journeying through Lent, completed chapters 3-24.

It seemed logical to keep going with Dr. Luke's fabulous story, and to move into his second volume, the Acts of the Apostles. Although this third book, *The Unquenchable Fire,* begins shortly before Pentecost, it can be used at any time.

The format is similar to the previous two guides. Although usable individually, it's ideally suited for groups, or congregations, where people are committed to work through it together. Many have suggested Luke's second volume could be listed in our Bibles as "the Acts of the Holy Spirit". It is God's story. At the core is the amazing narrative of how God established the church through Jesus' continuing activity by the Holy Spirit. It is a dynamic account of God at work in the world among his people.

As you read, remember that apart from brief glimpses in the New Testament epistles, this is the only Scriptural record we have of these unique events. From Jerusalem, within a generation, the gospel reaches the very heart of the Roman empire. This is a thrilling read. We have four gospels, but only one book of Acts; thank God for Dr. Luke, whose interest in these events, and his desire to inform his good friend Theophilus, caused him to investigate and communicate what we find here.

On the day of Pentecost, the Holy Spirit descended with tongues of fire upon the group of believers gathered in that Jerusalem house. They spilled out into the street. The fire spread, and continues spreading today. Nothing could quench it then, or now. The last chapter in this amazing story is yet to be written, when Jesus returns, as he has promised. We are part of this story. The very act of reading and exploring Dr. Luke's account of those early days in the life of the church, of praying through it, and of putting into practice what the Holy Spirit enlivens in us, draws us into this great story, our story, God's story. The fire of Pentecost is not the warming fire of a domestic log-burner, but the uncontainable, unquenchable fire of the Holy Spirit. Let it burn!

John G. Greenshields, Easter 2023.

ACKNOWLEDGEMENTS

The main Bible version used in this devotional guide is the 1987 New International Version (NIV), published by Hodder & Stoughton; others versions include the anglicised New Living Translation (NLT), published by Tyndale House Publishers in 2000, and the English Standard Version (ESV) produced by Crossway Bibles in 2008.

The illustrations used throughout the book are the work of Nyomi Lee Purves, to whom I am greatly indebted.

THE UNQUENCHABLE FIRE

Day 1 — Acts1:1-5 — Jerusalem

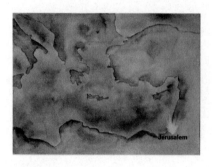

In his first volume (Luke's Gospel), the author had recounted to his friend Theophilus all that Jesus began to do and teach. Now we are presented with the clear implication that this same Jesus did not stop working following his earthly life. His work continues throughout the period covered by Acts, as it does in our world today.

Before finally leaving his followers, the risen Lord appears to them over a period of 40 days, speaking consistently about the kingdom of God. We can scarcely imagine what it must have been like to be present on such occasions. Envisage the risen Lord, right beside you, speaking and teaching as you drink in all that he says, amid the sheer wonder of his presence. "His word spoken before his suffering, spoken during his suffering and betrayal, is now the same word he speaks. He watches over his word to perform it…Jesus will continue his lessons for life for his disciples through the Spirit…Jesus speaks of the reign of God, a reign that has begun in his body."[1]

If that seems somewhat other-Sworldly, then consider v4: "as he was eating a meal with them" (NLT). Table fellowship with Jesus had been such a significant part of his time with his apostles during his three year ministry, and it didn't end after his resurrection. Here is a foretaste of the wedding supper of the Lamb (Revelation 19:7-10), a further powerful example of the humility of our risen Lord, and his love for his people.

Which of them could ever forget Jesus' words during that meal together, to wait in Jerusalem for the gift promised by his Father, the gift of being baptised with the Holy Spirit? Their expectations must have been raised; their anticipation heightened; yet mixed with unspoken questions. When

---

[1] Willie James Jennings, *Acts: A Theological Commentary on the Bible*, Westminster John Knox Press, pages 13-14

would this happen? How would they know? What exactly would it mean? Why wait when there was such good news to share? "The mission command provides direction for the church, and the Spirit gives the enablement."[2]

Going further...

- Why was it so important for Jesus' apostles to wait for the coming of the Holy Spirit? Christians are often activists, eager to get stuck into what needs to be done in demonstration and pursuit of the kingdom of God. When and why is it right to wait, and how does that address our sometimes frenetic lifestyles?

- Without Jesus and his work, we cannot make sense of the church's existence and activity. A visiting preacher in our church once set us a probing question: "What is there in this church that can only be explained by saying 'God did this'?" How would you answer?

Use Ian White's song as a simple prayer today —

> *Power from on high, power from on high,*
> *Lord, we are waiting for power from on high...*

---

2 Darrell L. Bock, *Acts*, Baker Academic 2007, page 56.

Day 2 — Acts 1:6-11

The question: v6

"Are we there yet?" Everyone who has travelled with young children will be familiar with that question. We know we are heading towards a destination, eager to get there, and that can easily spill over into impatience.

In different ways the question asked by Jesus' apostles has featured throughout the story of the Christian church. Sadly it has led to unwarranted claims regarding the second coming of Jesus, and endless, unproductive speculation regarding the end times. The words of the risen Lord in response should be read and received with humility and obedience. To paraphrase…

* "That's the Father's decision"

* "Your task is to be my witnesses, by the power of the Holy Spirit"

* "Begin where you are, and go to the ends of the earth"

The gospel is not just for the Jewish people, but for all the peoples of the world. Jesus' mission is global. Is that how we think? "The church exists, in major part, to extend the apostolic witness to Jesus everywhere. In fact, the church does not *have* a mission: it is to be missional and *is* a mission."[3]

This plan was not dreamed up by the church, but gradually revealed by God. Jesus' commission in these verses is the last thing he does on earth before his ascension, demonstrating how important it is.

The ascension: v9-11

Only Luke records details of the actual ascension of Jesus, coupled here with the angelic promise: "this Jesus…will come in the same way as you have seen him go into heaven" (v11, ESV). The assurance of his return simultaneously affirms the completion of the divine plan; meanwhile the church is called to engage in mission to the world.

"The ascension was the acknowledgement by the Father of the finished work of the Son. It set the stage for the

---

[3]Darrell L. Bock, referring to A. B. Robinson and R. W. Wall, *Called to be Church: The Book of Acts for a New Day*, 2006, pages 43-45.

sending of the Spirit. Taken with the truth set forth in 1:1, it implies a continuing concern for this world, which is made explicit in 1:11."[4]

Colin Sterne's hymn *We've a Story to Tell to the Nations* has this repeated refrain -

For the darkness shall turn to dawning,
and the dawning to noonday bright,
and Christ's great kingdom
shall come on earth,
the kingdom of love and light.[5]

Going further...

- "The church does not *have* a mission...it *is* a mission." If that's true, how should it affect us in our view of the church, our practices and participation in mission?

- Why is the ascension of Jesus so important?

---

[4] Everett F. Harrison, Acts, the Expanding Church, Moody Bible Institute, page 42

[5] Colin Sterne (1862-1926)

Day 3 — Acts 1:12-26

The upper room: v12-14

Jesus had commanded them to wait. We sometimes wait impatiently, twiddling our thumbs as we hope things will change. Sometimes we decide we've waited long enough. Yet to "wait on the Lord" is never pointless nor fruitless. When accompanied by united, fervent prayer, it becomes incredibly meaningful and productive.

In that upper room were gathered the eleven apostles, some unnamed women, plus Jesus' mother Mary and his brothers. This is the first reference to his younger brothers as believers. The only times we read of them in the gospels, they seem intent on dragging Jesus home from his itinerant ministry, perhaps embarrassed by his words and actions, even hostile towards him. Now they are united with the apostles and women, gathered to wait for the coming of the Holy Spirit, and they are praying… "with one accord devoting themselves to prayer."

Going further...

* If you have often prayed for friends or family without any tangible signs of change, be encouraged as you consider Jesus' brothers. It seems that God used the resurrection to impact their lives; pray for God to reveal his risen Son to those you love and lift before the Father.

* What do you think was their focus as they prayed? What can we learn from them?

Replacing Judas: v13-26

Jesus has ascended. His followers are united in prayer. Peter begins to emerge as a significant leader amongst this group. He takes the initiative in proposing that a replacement be appointed to take the place of Judas, whose gruesome death is vividly recorded, just as the position abdicated by his betrayal was predicted in two Old Testament prophetic Psalms — 69:25 and 109:8. Peter's conclusion in v21 is that someone should be chosen to take Judas' place. After two names are suggested and they pray together, lots are used to determine which one will become the 12th. apostle. It's Matthias — the only time, like his fellow nominee Barsabbas, that he is mentioned in the New Testament.

Was their method of choosing Matthias appropriate? This is the last time in the New Testament that lots are cast to determine God's will; once the Holy Spirit comes, such methods are never used again.

This story raises many questions. What prompted Peter's action? Why was it so important to have 12 apostles, all eyewitnesses of Jesus?

Is there an argument that Paul should have been the 12th. apostle, or was his situation a special exception?

Going further...

However we understand this section, there are helpful lessons we can grasp...

* Commit all your decisions to God in prayer, earnestly looking for his way

* Seek to discern together as God's people, drawing in the whole community: v15 says 120 were present, comprising 11 apostles, many others named in v13-14 and many unnamed believers.

* Give thanks for the gift of the Spirit, our divine Comforter and Guide.

Day 4 Acts 2:1-13

The day of Pentecost
Sometimes it's called the church's birthday, the community created by the Spirit. To the first century Jews it was the second annual harvest festival, 50 days after Passover. Suddenly God powerfully breaks into the natural rhythm, the daily ritual, of the spiritual life of these early believers in a dynamic way.

He sends the Holy Spirit, as promised in Luke 24:49 and Acts 1:4-5. His coming will enable the mission of God's people as given in Luke 24:47 and Acts 1:8. Here, being "filled with the `Holy Spirit" (v4) is related to proclaiming the gospel, equipping the church for mission, bringing salvation and transformed lives. Three phenomena are noted as these followers of Jesus are filled with the Holy Spirit…

1. The sound of a wind from heaven: this is clearly God's work, reminiscent of Jesus' words about the Holy Spirit being free, like the wind (John 3:8). We can neither control the Holy Spirit nor determine where and how he will operate. But we can be caught up in the force of his mighty power. Normally we hear storms raging outside; not this one, it's sound filled the house where they were gathered.

2. Divided tongues of fire: we are at the limits of human language. How can you possibly, adequately describe something so different, so powerful, so communal and yet so personal? All those present can really say is that it

was like tongues of fire, resting on each person in that room.

3. Speaking in other tongues: in this instance these were known languages, as soon becomes apparent, the purpose of which is to make known "the mighty works of God" (v11). To whom? To those in Jerusalem from all over the civilised world, amazingly listening to the gospel being shared in their own native languages, possibly even their own dialects. "God is bringing the message of the gospel home to those who hear it."[6]

God's mission is now well and truly underway. It is God's mission: these events were never planned or orchestrated by the new-born church. All they could do, and what we must also seek to do, is identify where he is at work and join him! He takes the initiative. He pours out the Holy Spirit. He enables and empowers his people. The message from Jerusalem will go out into all the world, as it is today. Jesus will build his church. Nothing can stop him. As the chorus says, "All over the world the Spirit is moving." The fire of the gospel is unquenchable.

---

[6] Bock, page 102.

Going further...

William Booth, founder of the Salvation Army, penned the words
from which the following hymn derives —

> *O God of burning cleansing flame*
> *Send the fire*
> *Your blood-bought gift today we claim*
> *Send the fire today*
> *Look down and see this waiting host*
> *And send the promised Holy Ghost*
> *We need another Pentecost*
> *Send the fire today*
> *Send the fire today*[7]

- "Send the fire today." If we sincerely and passionately pray this
  prayer, what do you think might happen?

- Where do you discern God the Holy Spirit at work? How can
  you co-operate with what he is doing?

---

[7] William Booth (1829-1912), adapted Lex Loizides © 1994 Kingsway's
Thankyou Music

Day 5 Acts 2:14-36

"Every sermon in Acts was an answer to a question."[8] That's worth pondering. Check it out as we move through Acts. Here there is no doubt. Chapter 2:12 lists the perplexing question demanding an answer. What was going on in the strange, miraculous phenomena being experienced? It's Peter, standing with the other eleven apostles, who answers.

Peter had denied Jesus during his trial, and wept bitterly as he departed from the scene (Luke 22:54-62). The same Peter had a personal encounter with the risen Lord; so personal that none of the details are recorded, save that it happened (1 Corinthians 15:5). He had been publicly restored by Jesus beside the Sea of Galilee (John 21:15-19). Now, empowered by the Holy Spirit, he resumes his leading role to answer the question voiced by the bewildered listeners. Daniel Bock asserts: "This speech is one of the most important theological declarations in the New Testament. It highlights who Jesus is and explains how one can know what God was doing through him."[9]

How does Peter answer the question in v12? Here is my attempt to summarise and paraphrase his sermon —
> v15: "They're not drunk... the pubs aren't open yet!"

> v16-21: "This fulfils what God said..." The last days the prophet Joel envisaged have now begun. The Spirit has been poured out. All who call upon the Lord will be saved.

> v22-35: "You crucified the Messiah, but God raised him up!"

> v36: The conclusion? "God has made this Jesus both Lord and Christ!"

Going further...

- What God was doing through the coming of the Holy Spirit prompted the question that led to Peter's sermon. Where is

---

[8] Dev. David Neil, Baptist Union of Scotland Mission Fieldworker, 1988-92.

[9] Bock, page 108

God at work today? What are the questions people are asking? Could contemporary sermons seek to give answers?

- Peter's answer began where people were, but led them inexorably to Jesus. Contemporary witnesses and preachers take note. Understanding more of who Jesus is, and introducing people to him, puts them in the place where God can work in significant ways in their lives. When you think of all Peter owed to his Lord, what else could he do...and what else can we do?

Child of our destiny,
God from eternity,
love of the Father on sinners outpoured;
see now what God has done
sending his only Son,
Christ the beloved One,
Jesus is Lord![10]

---

[10] © Timothy Dudley-Smith, *Name of all Majesty,* verse 3.

Day 6 Acts 2:37-47

"Lord and Messiah"

A phrase I have come to dislike intensely is the invitation to "make Jesus Lord of your life." We've probably all heard it or used it, usually well-intentioned. It's heresy is the notion that we can somehow elevate Jesus to the position of Lordship. We can't. God has already done this, decisively and permanently. That is Peter's conclusion to his sermon we read yesterday (v36 "God has made him both Lord and Messiah"). The real issue is how we respond to what God has done.

Peter is not allowed to end his sermon with yesterday's conclusion. Conviction settles upon the listeners, who press Peter to help them as the enormity of what they have done is realised; they were "cut (stabbed) to the heart" (v37). Is that it? Will God's judgement now fall in light of what they have done? Are we irretrievably lost?

There is hope!

Peter spells it out in v38-40...

• What they must do — repent and be baptised in the name of Jesus Christ, the crucified and risen Lord.

• What God will do — forgive them, bestow upon them the gift of the Holy Spirit, the same gift granted hours earlier to the first followers of Jesus, and bring them into his family.

• And the response? Quite staggering, with thousands of people receiving Peter's word and being baptised. One writer reckons that there could well have been 200,000 people in Jerusalem at that time, gathered for the Jewish Feast of Pentecost, 50 days after Passover. Perhaps 30,000 or more were able to hear Peter's words. Already Jesus' prediction in Acts 1:8 is coming true, with multitudes confessing Him as Lord...

Jesus! My shepherd, brother, friend,
my Prophet, Priest and King;
my Lord, my life, my way, my end,
accept the praise I bring.[11]

---

[11] John Newton (1725-1807), *How sweet the Name of Jesus sounds*, v4

"The church as it was meant to be"

"There were added that day about 3,000 souls." Added to what? To the group of disciples. The day of Pentecost is sometimes called the church's birthday. What is the church? How is it described? What makes it truly the church? It's God's new, called-out community, gathered by the Holy Spirit into and around the Lord Jesus Christ, through repentance and baptism in(to) his name.

In times when loose language is used to talk about the church, its life and mission, these verses in Acts are of great significance. When the late J. B. Philips was working on his New Testament translation, he was gripped by these verses. After studying them, reflecting on them at length and translating them, he wrote these words: "We cannot help feeling disturbed as well as moved, for this is surely the church as it was meant to be. It is vigorous and flexible, for these are the days before it ever became fat and short of breath through prosperity, or muscle-bound by over-organisation…if they were uncomplicated and naive by modern standards we have ruefully to admit that they were open on the Godward side…"[12]

v42: Their core life — devoted to the apostles' teaching and fellowship, the breaking of bread and prayer. All of life, in all its levels, is encapsulated here. Problems will inevitably emerge (as in chs. 5-6) yet if bound together in Christ, we can keep on growing through them.

v43: Their expectation — of God at work. Nothing quickens faith more than experiencing and witnessing the transforming power of God.

v44-45: Their commitment — to God and to one another; not a required communalism, but a voluntary caring and sharing.

v46-47: Their growth — both spiritual and numerical. "Around 3,000" is further augmented as 2:47 shows, to be followed by other similar references, in Acts 4:4, 4:32-33, 6:1&7, 8:4-8, 9:31, and 11:19-21.

---

[12] J. B. Philips, quoted in *The Radical Christian*, by Arthur Wallis, page 112.

Going further...

- We live in a different time and context, yet we are also part of the great kingdom movement of God by his Spirit in the world, and through his people, the church of the living God. What principles do we recognise in the life of this earliest church in Acts? What can we adapt and apply in our life together today? Talk and pray about this in your group, and see where the Holy Spirit leads you!

- Why was/is repentance and baptism so significant as we turn to Jesus?

- What does it mean for us today to "devote" ourselves as these new believers did (v42)?

Day 7 Acts 3:1-10

Peter and John went to pray, they met a lame man
on the way;
he asked for alms and held out his palms,
and this is what Peter did say:

Silver and gold have I none, but such as I have give
I thee.
In the name of Jesus Christ of Nazareth,
rise up and walk!

The unknown author who penned these words has forever embedded today's story from Acts in the minds of a generation who learned to sing it as well as read it. And why not? It celebrates and reflects this first of 14 apostolic miracles recorded in Acts. It's a great story, with some hidden depths.

v1: For example, the continuance of these apostles with the daily prayers offered at the Jerusalem Temple, as 2:46 has already stated. The ninth hour would be 3pm. Breaking with the Jewish religion would happen gradually, and the early believers saw no immediate need to sever their ties. On the contrary, they are frequently found in or around the temple, sharing in daily worship and prayer. Yet Acts chapters 3-5 also show the growing tensions and rising opposition of the temple authorities to this new movement.

Peter and John are often together in the stories from the gospels and Acts. See John 18:15-17 (Peter's denial of Jesus), John 20:2-8 (the resurrection), John 21: 18-22

(Jesus' future predictions), Acts 4:13 &19, and 8:14-23.

v4: "Look at us." When eye contact is made, something happens. Most people would no doubt walk past this man, avoiding eye contact, conscious only of his hand stretched out, asking for alms. Peter and John stop and fix their gaze upon this man.

"Look at us." Does God give the two apostles insight to know what must be said next? Is faith awakened in this man? When we meet people in need, do we really see them, or look past them? What might be achieved in the name of Jesus if we ask God to enable us to see with his eyes, and stop to engage needy people in a deeply meaningful way?

v6: The miracle of the lame man's healing occurs "in the name of Jesus Christ of Nazareth," invoking the Lord's presence and power. "The gate of the temple becomes the entrance to a new future. Peter and John have entered that future, and now they perform it."[13]
Although not physically present, Jesus is still active by the Holy Spirit through the apostles he has chosen, equipped, commissioned and empowered. Now, working through them, this lame man's life is completely transformed.

Going further...

- Peter and John had been fishermen together, probably business partners, and early followers of Jesus. Their friendship endured as they grew closer to Jesus, and to one another. Thank God for those people who have been close to you for many years, and helped you to follow Jesus. Consider one way you could encourage someone else today.

- "Compassion expresses itself in service to others and in meeting their needs."[14] How do we respond to people in need, for example when we pass people begging in the streets? How should we respond?

---

[13] Jennings, page 40.

[14] Bock, page 158.

Day 8 Acts 3:11-4:4

Yesterday we celebrated the first apostolic miracle recorded in Acts. Now comes the aftermath. The miracle creates a great stir in the temple precincts, as people wonder what has happened, and how it has come about. Cue the second great opportunity for Peter to deliver an impromptu sermon.

v12-16: It's not an easy sermon for the listeners. Peter points unerringly to God's work through the Lord Jesus Christ as the divine source of this man's healing and transformation. Yet he also declares the guilt of his listeners in the condemnation and crucifixion of Jesus. "You disowned the Holy and Righteous One…you killed the author of life" (v15)! The gospel is good news, but before we can embrace it we must know the truth about our own sinfulness and need, however unwelcome that might be.

v17-26: Still there is hope. If conviction condemns, genuine repentance opens the door to the grace of God and inner renewal, in anticipation of God's final restoration planned through the return of Jesus

from heaven. All of this is in line with what God has already spoken through the Old Testament prophets.

Peter preaches Jesus from the Old Testament; now Jesus has been received into heaven until the time of his return, when all God's promises will be completed. Meanwhile the healing of this lame man can be fully explained through the power of the name of Jesus, the risen, ascended, reigning Lord.

4:1-4: Repercussions follow. The temple authorities appear, annoyed by the proclamation of Jesus' resurrection by both these apostles. The Sadduccees, who represented the privileged elite, working with the Roman overlords, denied the whole idea of resurrection, although most other Jews did believe in it. The apostles are arrested and imprisoned…and yet many receive their message and believe, in the region of 5,000 men. The incredible catalogue of Christian growth continues; from 120 (1:15), plus 3,000 (2:41) and now 5,000 more. The unquenchable fire is spreading.

Jesus is Lord! O'er sin the mighty conqueror,
from death he rose and all his foes shall own His name.
Jesus is Lord! God sends His Holy Spirit
to show by works of power that Jesus is Lord.[15]

Going further...

- This sermon is rich in Christology, reflecting on Jesus' identity and person. What can we learn from how he is portrayed in 3:13-15, 18 & 22, and how does this impact our lives?

- Look again at 3:26, where Peter speaks of God's blessing coming through "turning ...from your wicked ways". Is there something you need to confess and repent of today? Do it now, and receive God's blessing.

- As we have noticed, Luke refers many times to the numerical growth of the number of believers (e.g. 4:4). Why does this matter, and what other signs of growth do you see in the story he carefully tells us?

---

[15] David Mansell © 1982 Word's Spirit of Praise Music/CopyCare

Day 9 Acts 4:5-22

After a night in jail, the authorities may think that the two errant apostles will come to their senses. When proceedings resume in the morning, however, Peter's words continue from where he left off the previous day, this time before the religious and civic heavyweights of Jerusalem.

The Council, the Sanhedrin, was the highest court in the land, consisting of 70 men drawn from the diverse strands within Judaism. As Peter and John are brought before them, Jesus' prediction in Mark 13:9 is fulfilled.

"No other name"
"Filled with the Holy Spirit," not the first or the last time this would be Peter's experience, he speaks directly to the Jewish leaders. Neither he nor John can take any credit for what has happened. The demonstration of God's power and kindness is directly attributed to Jesus Christ of Nazareth, the only one in whom salvation can be found. Where else can we discover such a potent mixture of divine power and kindness?

En-couraged (v13), Peter and John confound the accusing leaders. None can deny their association with Jesus, nor the miracle that has taken place. And none can cow them or silence them, in spite of warnings and threats (v18 & 21). Peter's closing words on this occasion include a statement that has brought help to countless numbers of believers through the centuries who have suffered for their faith in Jesus (v19-20). Our first duty is always to obey God; should that conflict with our duty to any other authority, our course of action is clear.

The Jewish leaders are amazed at the boldness, directness, and confidence of Peter and John, recognising them as men who had been with Jesus. Perhaps some recalled them from that awful night of Jesus' trial, when John remained silent, and Peter denied Jesus (John 18:15-27). Now they appear before the council as men transformed, witnessing fearlessly to the rejected and resurrected Jesus.

Christ the Cornerstone
Peter's quotation from Psalm 118:22, in v11, may well be at the centre of this passage in Acts. The Jewish leaders are struggling to maintain their

hold over their people. Failing to recognise Jesus ("the stone you builders rejected") does not stop God exalting him as the cornerstone of the 'building' he is creating in his people. "In the Old Testament, God had a temple for his people. Now in the New Testament he has a people for his temple."[16]

Going further...

* In a pluralistic society, Peter's claim in v12 is exclusive, and regarded by some as an incendiary comment. "Don't all religions lead to God?" "As long as people are sincere, surely that's what matters?" "What if you narrow-minded Christians are wrong?" Talk in your group about how you respond to such questions.

* Imagine you are the healed man in his 40s, standing there while the Council deliberates (v14 & 22). What would you want to say?

* Most of us may not have to face the dilemma of weighing obedience to God against obedience to the state or other authority...or have we? Ask that question in your group, and pray for all today who are called to witness to Jesus in a hostile environment.

> *Jesus, the name high over all,*
> *in hell, or earth, or sky:*
> *angels and men before it fall,*
> *and demons fear and fly.*
>
> *Jesus, the name to sinners dear,*
> *the name to sinners given;*
> *it scatters all their guilty fear,*
> *it turns their hell to heaven.*[17]

---

[16] Rev. Jim Graham, late of Goldhill Baptist Church, Bucks.

[17] Charles Wesley (1707-88)

Day 10 Acts 4:23-31

Following their release, Peter and John return "to their own people" (v23 NIV). Is Luke beginning to emphasise the distinction now between their ethnic and religious identity, and their new DNA as the redeemed and gathered people of God? After giving their report, the community pray together. What a prayer meeting! Note the following strands in their prayers...

"Sovereign Lord"

There is no doubt in their minds that God is sovereign over all that is happening, even using the opposition of the Jewish leaders to bring about his will. Quoting from Psalm 2:1-2, they acknowledge the futility of all who oppose God, doomed to failure. "The futility of human opposition to God is never seen to better advantage than when it serves to implement his plan."[18]

We need to recapture that same confidence these early believers shared, expressed in that simple, but incredibly powerful and profound phrase, "Sovereign Lord." That's where our prayers should truly begin, as Jesus himself taught us in the Lord's Prayer in Matthew 6:9-13.

Their petitions

They don't pray for safety, nor freedom from suffering or persecution, nor vindication before the Council, nor judgement upon those opposing them. The believers are concerned that they might speak God's word with boldness, and see God's power at work in healings and miracles through the name of Jesus. Their requests stand in marked contrast to our prayers that can often be self-centred rather than kingdom-focussed.

The outcome

When God is powerfully at work, there are often physical phenomena that manifest his presence. On this occasion we read that the building shook, they were all filled with the Holy Spirit (again!), and spoke the word of God boldly. Despite the warnings received from the Council, they had a passion to share what God had done through Jesus.

---

[18] Everett F. Harrison, *Acts - The Expanding Church*, Moody Press, Chicago, page 89.

Going further...

- What can we learn from these early believers about praying together? Talk about this in your group, but make sure you also pray — far too often I have spoken with others about prayer, and yet we never actually prayed!

- Are manifestations of God's powerful presence linked to our prayers? If so, how should we pray?

Day 11 Acts 4:32-37

As we have already seen, Luke periodically summarises how the gospel spread and how the church grew. Here is another of these fascinating insights. The twin emphases here are on the continuing power of God at work through apostolic proclamation, and the dynamic impact of realised fellowship. It's that second aspect of their common life we focus on today. Community life involves mission and mutual care.

A united people

They are described as being "one in heart and mind" (v32). Out of this common life emerges a willingness to share whatever they have. Psalm 133 recognises and celebrates the blessings that come when God's people "live together in unity." This unity is manifested in a willingness to live faithfully and share freely, out of loving concern for others.

Voluntary and generous giving

Only once have I heard a contemporary story of someone selling their home in order to provide for others. In the case in point, it was to provide a home for an evangelist so he and his family could be supported while he fulfilled his ministry. It echoes what we read in v34-35. This was not a form of communism, as some have implied, nor an enforced practice. Entirely voluntary, those who chose to sell property and provide for others did so out of a response to the grace of God impacting their lives (v33). The noted example of Barnabas ("Son of encouragement") highlights their loving response to God, and their loving commitment to one another.

Later we will read about Paul organising a collection to support poor believers in Jerusalem. There are some suggestions that the practice of selling houses referred to here may inadvertently have led to poverty and necessitated the later collection. That could well be so, yet it does not invalidate the heartfelt response of these Jerusalem believers to support brothers and sisters in need.

Going further...

- Are there ways in which we can follow the example of these early believers? Consider that with others as you reflect on this passage.

- What promotes unity amongst God's people, and what blessings arise from it? Pray as Jesus prayed. See John 17:20-23.

- Find out more about Barnabas, mentioned 23 times in Acts, one of Luke's heroes.

There is a place of commanded blessing,
where brethren in unity dwell
A place where anointing oil is flowing
where we'll live as one.
You have called us to be a body,
You have called us as friends
Joined together in the bond of Your Spirit
unto the end.
Father, we join in the prayer of Jesus;
as You are so let us be one,
Joined together in unity and purpose,
all for the love of Your Son
We will break dividing walls,
we will break dividing walls
in the name of Your Son,
We will break dividing walls...
...we will be one[19]

---

[19] David Francis Ruis, © 1993 Mercy/Vineyard Publishing

Day 12 Acts 5:1-11

There's a story in Greek mythology of a character named Icarus, given wings by his father and warned not to fly too close to the sun. Icarus ignores the warning, and as a consequence the wax in his wings melts and he comes to a sticky end. It's only a myth, yet has some parallel with today's reading. So too does F. W. Faber's hymn...

My God, how wonderful thou art!
Thy majesty how bright!
How beautiful Thy mercy-seat,
In depths of burning light!

How wonderful, how beautiful,
The sight of Thee must be,
Thine endless wisdom, boundless power,
and awesome purity![20]

Faber moves from thinking about God's holiness and goes on to rejoice in the wonder of his love for sinful human beings. Yet it's his words on God's holy character that help us consider this story.

The previous action of Barnabas (4:36-37), and the editorial comment of 4:32, sets the scene. The deception of Ananias and Sapphira was totally unnecessary, as Peter points out in v4. Having decided to sell their property, they were free to give or keep as much as they wished; their deceit lay in falsely pretending to give the whole proceeds.

Lying to God, with feigned generosity, may have been planned to impress others, or put this couple in a more honourable place within the church fellowship, yet it all backfires disastrously.

How does this story impact us? Should we live in abject fear of the holy God who sees what is deep within our hearts? Can we approach him in sincerity without being scared of his judgement? Or is the real lesson from this tragic couple more to do with our need to "walk in the light" (1 John 1:5-10)? To be open and real with God, and with others? To

---

[20] F. W. Faber, 1814-63

stop pretending about ourselves or our actions? To accept responsibility for how we use the resources God has given us? And to affirm that God's grace is bestowed upon us when we are true to him, not when we try to fool him?

Luke's closing comment in this section (v11) speaks about the impact this story has on the entire church[21]. The Holy Spirit is present in our life together. He is witness to the deepest intentions within our hearts. He scrutinises our motives as well as observing our actions. He is holy, and he wants us to be holy too. Sin must be dealt with.

In the words of the Narnian character Mr. Beaver, trying to describe Aslan to the children who have not yet heard of him — "Safe? Who said anything about him being safe? Of course he's not safe; but he's good. He's the King, I tell you."

Going further...

- Note the lurking danger in v3, where Peter recognises Satan's influence upon this couple. "Most New Testament references to Satan's activity relate to saints rather than to the unbelieving world."[22] What steps can we take to guard against his influence upon us?

- God sees and knows all that is happening in us. Let's seek to walk in the light, and be filled daily with the Holy Spirit. Here's a useful and powerful prayer...

"Search me, O God, and know my heart,
test me and know my thoughts.
Point out anything in me that offends you,
and lead me along the path of everlasting life"[23]

---

[21] Church = ekklesia; this is the first of 23 specific uses of this word in Acts.

[22] Everett F. Harrison, page 93.

[23] Psalm 139:23-24, New Living Translation

Day 13 Acts 5:12-16

Fear and faith

My friend Ronnie was both a postman and a pastor. One day in the sorting office a colleague commented that the Bible was full of contradictions. Ronnie took out a £5 note and offered it to him if he could identify one; Ronnie's money was safe! Yet today there seems to be a direct contradiction in successive verses 13 & 14. In the light of yesterday's reading, how could the same church community live in "great fear" (v11) that seems to have made people reluctant to join, and yet have "more and more men and women" believing in the Lord (v14)?

Willie James Jennings puts it well: "Like the people of Israel at the foot of Mount Sinai, where holy space was touched and someone died, so too now fear grips the followers. Yet much like life at the foot of the mountain, so too again we find crowds of broken and needy people looking for the power of God to touch them." [24]

"Sovereign Lord...stretch out your hand..." (4:24 & 30)

In this latest reflection on the story thus far, Dr. Luke presents a vivid summary of the amazing acts of the Holy Spirit. He simultaneously portrays a divinely inspired sense of awe, even as many are drawn irresistibly to faith in the Lord Jesus Christ.

The healing miracles described in v15-16 bear further testimony to this astonishing time, as the Holy Spirit is poured out upon the followers of Jesus, and those amongst whom they live and work. People flock into Jerusalem, to Solomon's Portico in the temple, bringing many sick and demonised people, and all are healed, even in ways we may well find extraordinary.

The apostles are instrumental in this ministry, these miraculous events accrediting them as Christ's representatives. The church is not organising or orchestrating this; the Holy Spirit is at work, and the believers are caught up in the wind and fire of God.

---

[24] Jennings, page 55.

Going further...

- Was the purging of sin referred to yesterday directly linked with the great manifestations of the power of God at work in today's reading? And are these events also connected to the prayers of 4:24-30? If so, what can we learn and apply?

- Commenting on the blessing and growth of his church, my pastor friend said: "We never planned any of this. We simply tried to see where God was at work and respond to what he was doing." In what areas do you see God at work in your church and community?

He longs to do much more than
our faith has yet allowed,
to thrill us and surprise us
with His sovereign power.
Where darkness has been darkest,
the brightest light will shine;
His invitation comes to us —
it's yours and it is mine...
...Come on in and taste the new wine,
the wine of the kingdom of God...[25]

---

[25] Graham Kendrick, *One shall tell another*, © 1981 Kingsway's Thankyou

Day 14 Acts 5:17-42

Jail and open doors: v17-24
Once more the apostles are arrested and spend a night in jail, or at least part of a night, thanks to the intervention of an angel who comes to release them. He simultaneously leaves the jail doors locked and intact, much to the consternation of the guards and chief priests! Chains and locked doors are no barrier to God. Nothing can stop the advance of the gospel.

Why were they jailed? See v25-28. Luke has already noted the element of jealousy motivating the high priest and his associates (v17). So once again Peter and the others are brought before the Sanhedrin and questioned by the high priest. Once more the accusers hear a message that is direct, convicting, and yet hopeful.

Threats and beatings: v33-40
Death threats follow, at which point the Pharisee Gamaliel steps in as the Sanhedrin goes into closed session. His logic is that if these men (the apostles) are acting purely on their own behalf, their cause is doomed to failure; however, if this is God's work, the Jewish leaders must not be seen opposing it. His argument prevails, yet before releasing the apostles they are flogged and ordered not to speak any more in the name of Jesus.

Joy and proclamation: v41-42
The outcome? They rejoice in their suffering, perhaps recalling Jesus' words in Matthew 5:11-12. They continue their proclamation, as instructed by the angel (v20), both in the temple, and from house to house.

This is one of the first references to the use of homes for gathering and sharing the good news. This will become increasingly important as the story of the church develops, so much so that early Christianity would become known as a home-based movement. The earliest known use of specific buildings for meeting together would not come for around another 100 years.

Going further...

- Discipleship involves suffering, even the prospect of violent death. This was the apostles' experience, and also that of many believers in our world today. Pray for those who are suffering for the sake of "the Name" (v41).

- Someone has said that the Christian church proportionately grew more in its first 150 years, without designated buildings, than it has ever done since. Are buildings a blessing or a hindrance? How can we make them more of a blessing in pursuing mission and ministry than a burden or a hindrance?

- "People won't find a home in the church until they find the church in the home."[26] What do you think, and how might this impact your church family?

---

[26] Anonymous quote. See Robert Banks, *Paul's Idea of Community*, Eerdmans, 1980.

Day 15 Acts 6:1-7

I've sometimes heard people bemoan the state of the contemporary church, longing to return to the days of the early church. OK, but which church? Corinth, with its issues of immorality and division? Ephesus, where the church had lost its first love? One of the Galatian churches, who had become very legalistic? And so on. What about the first church, in Jerusalem? That would be great, or would it?

We read today of one of the significant problems faced by the Jerusalem church. Growth brings blessings and problems too. Conflicts will inevitable arise where saved sinners are gathered together into the new people of God. That should not surprise us. What really matters is how we deal with the problems when they emerge. Let me suggest a positive pattern for responding based on Acts 6:1-7.

- **They recognised the problem,** and faced up to it. Hellenistic Jews, either from outside Palestine, and/or whose first language was Greek, complained that their widows were being neglected as daily help was being distributed (see 4:34-35).

- **They (the apostles) gathered the disciples together,** and offered helpful guidance. The whole community seems to have been involved in the process, without diminishing the role of the apostolic leaders in offering direction.

- **They established a clear principle**. The key functions of the apostles (prayer and the ministry of the word) must not be impinged upon by added responsibilities. And yet…

- **They saw the importance of caring** for needy and vulnerable people within the church community. This was never questioned; the real issue was how to enable it to happen without holding back the progress of the gospel.

- **They reached consensus** about how to move forward. Thus the unity of the church was maintained, and the Lord's name honoured.

- **They delegated responsibility** to seven men

who would take over this role. The criteria used to determine appropriate people (ethical, spiritual and practical) are reflected in the later pastoral epistles, eg 1 Timothy 3. Their role was a spiritual one, hence the need to be "full of the Spirit and wisdom," and to be set apart with prayer and the laying on of hands.

- **Their action led to further blessing.** As God's word increased, and disciples multiplied in number, that included "a great many of the priests" (v7).

A situation that could have led to a damaging split along ethnic lines in this young church was averted. God was glorified, and the Jerusalem church continued to grow.

We usually run from conflict. Yet, faced with God's help, it can be a blessing in disguise. It can become an opportunity for the Christian church to demonstrate that the gospel we proclaim really does work. With the Spirit's help we can face the issues and work through them in a gracious, life-affirming way. Maybe, if you wanted to join a new Testament church, Jerusalem is not a bad choice!

Going further...

- The care of widows and orphans is highlighted in the New Testament, here and elsewhere, eg James 1:27 and I Timothy 5:3-10. Where is the greatest need in your church community today? How could you respond? Talk and pray with your group about this.

- What are the key roles of pastors/ministers? If we believe that all God's people are equipped to serve him, what can be devolved to others to help our leaders focus on their key tasks?

> Build Your Church, Lord,
> make us strong, Lord,
> join our hearts, Lord, through Your Son;
> make us one, Lord, in Your body,
> in the kingdom of Your Son[27]

27 Dave Richards, *For I'm building a people of power*, © 1977 Kingsway's Thankyou Music

Day 16 Acts 6:8-7:1

Of the seven men appointed to oversee distribution of aid to widows and dependents (6:5), two will feature significantly in Acts — Philip and Stephen. It's Stephen's story that features over the next few days.

His appointment to aid relief work is just the start of his ministry. Soon we see evidence of the widespread impact of the Holy Spirit upon his life. His administrative abilities and compassionate care are augmented by miraculous deeds, coming from this man who is described as being "full of grace and power." What a wonderful combination. Grace without power may seem insipid, lacklustre; power without grace can lead to domination and tyranny. Grace and power combined is reminiscent of the Lord Jesus himself, as portrayed in John 1:14-18.

To these indisputable qualities you can add apologetic ability, ie. being able to handle public debate, equipped with divinely-inspired words that display true wisdom.

Stephen's words ring true, and his insight is clear. Yet there is a cost; truth embitters those whom it does not enlighten. Soon opposition to him gathers momentum, with false accusations of blasphemy, as Stephen is brought before the council, the Sanhedrin. In that pressure cauldron, effectively on trial for his life, his face reflects the very radiance of God, "like the face of an angel" (v15), the only time this phrase is used in the New Testament.

Going further...

- Do we sometimes consign people to one particular task, without expecting or looking for significant development in their lives as God works in and through them? What Stephens are there among us that we need to encourage and support?

- God's work in Stephen highlights two things — that the apostles were glad to share ministry with others, and that all God's people are equipped by the Holy Spirit to serve. How are you serving the Lord today?

- What do you see in Stephen's character that helped facilitate God's powerful work in him?

Day 17

Before your read the Bible passage…

…Today's reading is longer than most; it's the longest speech in Acts. Pease don't speed through it, but listen carefully to this sermon, the final earthly words of the first Christian martyr. Note the two main themes — (1) the leaders God raised up who were not recognised, and (2) the failure of Israel, God's people, to follow him, descending instead into repeated disobedience and idolatry. As the story of Stephen's trial and death unfolds, there are many similarities with the experience of Jesus. See how many connections you can make as you read through this chapter. *Now read Acts 7:2-60*

Stand up for Stephen

See v55-56. After his ascension, Jesus is described as being seated at the right hand of God the Father (Colossians 3:1 & Hebrews 8:1). The only place where he is described as standing is here, as Stephen is stoned to death. Commenting on this, the late Tom Smail borrowed and amended a line from an old hymn — "Stand up, stand up for Stephen."[28] The Lord Jesus stands to welcome and receive his faithful martyred servant. The condemnation of Stephen in the earthly court is in sharp contrast to his vindication in the court of heaven.

This is the third trial (actually here it's more like mob justice) recorded in Acts. Luke has told us previously of the warnings (4:21) that moved on to beatings (5:40) and now to death. Witnessing faithfully can be very costly, yet full of the promise of heavenly reward.

Stephen's final words

Against the deeply touching background, and the heavenly welcome afforded to Stephen, it might seem rather churlish to explore his 'sermon' to the Jewish leaders. Yet it is revealing. It demonstrates Stephen's grasp of the story of the people of Israel, and the crucial God-inspired events that shaped their history and defined them as the people of God. Stephen's words in effect refute the charges laid against him (see 6:11-14), as he spends some time reflecting on God's word and work

---

[28] Adapted from the hymn *Stand up, stand up for Jesus*; used at the conference on *The Power of Love and the Love of Power*, Aberdeen in late 1990s.

through Moses and Jesus. It also exposes the repeated failures of God's people to listen to the voice of God and obey what he had said. It's this aspect of the sermon that infuriates the listeners, who are enraged at Stephen's application of the truths underlying the Old Testament drama. Luke tells us their reaction in v57.

Responding to an unwelcome message

Before we condemn them, perhaps we should ask how often we have done the same. Do we ever choose not to hear when God speaks unwelcome words, even if they are true? How many times have we raised our voices to drown out the voice of God? "It is a particularly powerful moment when Scripture is applied in such a way that it exposes what is really going on."[29] This is uncomfortable reading, and yet the corollary is that if we truly and sincerely humble ourselves before God, and receive his word to us, it leads us into his grace and mercy revealed supremely in Jesus.

Stephen's last action is to pray for forgiveness for his executioners. One significant bystander, complicit in the mob violence that resulted in Stephen's death, is a young man named Saul. That final prayer of Stephen is heard in heaven, and how it would be answered!

For all the saints who from their labours rest,
who Thee by faith before the world confessed,
Thy Name, O Jesu, be for ever blest,
Alleluia![30]

Going further

- It can be deeply challenging, and profoundly unsettling, when God's words are directly applied to our lives. How can we guard against hard-heartedness, and maintain a right relationship and proper responsiveness to God?

- See v48-50. Do we ever try to "contain" God? What can we learn from Stephen?

---

[29] Bock, page 306.

[30] William Walshaw How (1823-97)

Day 18 Acts 8:1-4

Fire in the grate

My father worked as a blacksmith for the National Coal Board. One of the few perks for these hard-working men at the pits (the only perk I remember!) was cheaper coal, so there was always a fire burning in our home. Keeping the burning coals confined in the grate was vital; occasionally when some inferior coal began sparking and spluttering badly, little bits would shoot out, landing on the carpet, and lead to prompt and furious activity to get them back into the grate and stop the fire spreading.

Today's reading reminds me of those childhood days. Following Stephen's death, the first great widespread wave of persecution breaks out in Jerusalem, resulting in many believers fleeing from the city, leaving the apostles behind. And the chief instigator of this oppression of the church? That young man Saul who looked after the coats of Stephen's executioners.

Since Stephen's death as the first martyr, millions more have suffered and died for their Lord. They have been, and should be, deeply mourned by godly people (v2), yet laid to rest in the glorious hope of resurrection. The mourning for Stephen ("loud weeping" NLT), may be an act of defiance and a statement of support for what Stephen said.

Persecution and scattering

What tough times for that young Christian church and its leaders. Jesus' words (see Matthew 24:9-14) are being fulfilled. Why the apostles stay behind in Jerusalem, possibly in hiding, is not made clear. SWas this a strategic plan, or had they misread the events unfolding around them? How did their actions fit into the prophetic plan envisaged by Jesus himself in Acts 1:8?

We don't know, yet we cannot escape the wonderful outcome even of this severe persecution. "The believers who had fled Jerusalem went everywhere preaching the good news about Jesus" (v4). If the devil had instigated that outburst of persecution, with Saul as the main perpetrator, his plan backfired. Instead of extinguishing the fire, the scattering of the disciples, like the burning coals, began multiple fires everywhere Jesus' followers went, spreading the good news about him. The fire of God cannot be quenched or contained!

Going further...

- The people God used to spread the good news were not the apostles, important though they were, but ordinary believers. How might he want to use you today? Pray for your witness where you are "scattered" each week.

> Let the song go round the earth,
> Jesus Christ is Lord!
> Sound His praises, tell His worth,
> be His name adored;
> every clime and every tongue
> join the glad, the glorious song![31]

---

[31] S G Stock (1838-98)

Day 19 Acts 8:5-25 — Samaria

"You will be my witnesses in Jerusalem, and in all Judea, and Samaria…" (Jesus speaking, in Acts 1:8). The unquenchable fire is spreading; persecution in Jerusalem had served to force believers out of the city. Luke's attention now turns to an unnamed city in Samaria, and the ministry of Philip (see 6:5) in that area. His willingness to go there is in itself highly significant, as we shall see.

Philip the evangelist: v5-13

Philip's ministry is attested by miraculous deliverances, healings, and conversions. Among those who believe the good news and are baptised is Simon the sorcerer, a powerful local figure whose previous career in magic is superseded by the amazing demonstration of the kingdom of God through Philip the evangelist.

Peter and John, the apostles: v14-17

This story raises some fascinating questions. Why was the Holy Spirit withheld until the apostles came and prayed with laying on of hands? Does this suggest a two-stage conversion experience, with faith subsequently confirmed by the gift of the Holy Spirt? That's how many Pentecostal Christians understand this passage.

There is an alternative. First century Palestinian society was deeply divided. One division was between monotheistic Jews and syncretistic Samaritans, ancient half-cousins and historical enemies (remember the story of the good Samaritan in Luke 10:25-37)?

Could it be that at such a significant time for the advance of God's kingdom, the visit from Peter and John, sent by the Jerusalem apostles, would serve to affirm that God wanted only one church? That the bestowal of the Holy Spirit to Samaritan believers emphasised they too were part of God's family, and so the way was being paved for Gentiles also to receive the gospel? That any prospect of a schism should be quelled, replaced by the sheer joy of seeing and knowing that the Holy Spirit was truly working in people of all ethnicities and religious backgrounds?

Difficulties emerge when we try to superimpose a particular conversion pattern from Acts and then make it into a doctrine. Luke wants us to be caught up in the wonder of the story he is telling, the freedom of the Holy Spirit to use people like Philip, Peter, and John, and to work as he wishes as the sovereign God. In these exceptional circumstances, the normative pattern of Acts 2:38-39 should be kept firmly in focus.

Simon the sorcerer: v18-25

Jealous of the apostles' apparent power to convey the Holy Spirit through prayer and laying on of hands, a new convert, Simon the erstwhile sorcerer, wants a bit of the action too. Can he buy into this supreme power? Peter gives him short shrift. You can't buy God's gift with money: those who peddle a prosperity gospel take note! Peter perceives Simon's heart is not right with God, and still captive to sin. Desire for power and misuse of money lead many to a spiritual fall.

Don't miss the importance and wonder of v25. Now convinced that Samaritans too can enter God's kingdom, Peter and John embark on a mini preaching tour of local villages. Don't forget that John once wanted to call down fire from heaven on a Samaritan village (Luke 9:54). Now a different fire is spreading there!

Going further...

- Was Simon truly converted? What do you think, and why? (Compare John 2:23-25).

- The gospel of the kingdom breaks down ancient barriers, uniting people under the Lordship of Jesus Christ. What divisions need to be challenged and changed today?

Holy Spirit, You are welcome here
Come flood this place and fill the atmosphere
Your glory, God, is what our hearts long for
To be overcome by Your presence, Lord[32]

---

[32] Bryan Torwalt, Katie Torwalt, Bryan James Torwalt, Katelin Michelle © 2011 Capital CMG Genesis, Jesus Culture Music

Day 20 Acts 8:26-40 — Gaza

God's ways: Philip appears in Acts as quite a remarkable and humble man. We first encounter him as one of the 7 men entrusted with distribution of aid in Acts 6:1-7; then find him actively spreading the good news in Samaria, with great effectiveness. He may have shared with Peter and John in the itinerant ministry concluding yesterday's reading (8:25). Now, perhaps strangely to us, an angel is sent to take Philip away from such a fruitful sphere of service and direct him to a desert location over 20 miles away, setting up a meeting with one man in particular. Surely it would have been better to let him continue his successful evangelism in Samaria? Why remove him from that and lead him to a barren location? God's ways are not our ways, and, to his credit, Philip obeys without question.

Up to now Acts has majored on mass conversions. Over the next few chapters, the emphasis shifts to individual stories, the more personal side of evangelism. All are the work of the Holy Spirit.

God's guidance: Initially guidance comes from an angel, then directly from the Spirit speaking to him (v29), then from the circumstances as he hears the Ethiopian official reading aloud from the book of Isaiah.

Philip's wisdom is shown in his sensitivity to this stranger. He starts where the man is in his scripture reading; he offers help in understanding; he responds to the question posed by the Ethiopian; and he leads him towards Jesus — the Servant of the Lord whose suffering was predicted by Isaiah. The subsequent baptism of this foreign eunuch confirms his conversion; he resumes his long journey home (probably around 1,000 miles) as a new person.

God's mission: Just as suddenly as he was directed to the desert road, Philip is taken away by the Spirit of the Lord. He was the right person in the right place at the right time, in a meeting initiated by God.

The outcome? A new believer travels back to North Africa, rejoicing in his new-found faith in Jesus. Who knows what the implications of that might be, as the gospel begins to reach to the ends of the earth?

Philip's ministry continues northwards along the Mediterranean coast until he reaches Caesarea. He is an outstanding example of an ordinary believer used by God to open up that whole coastal area to the gospel. He is faithful, going wherever directed by God, ready to share Jesus and explain the good news to anyone willing to listen: a good model for us to imitate.

Going further...

- We might describe Philip's experience here as a divine appointment. Have you had one? Share it with your group, or with a friend, and reflect on how that experience affected you as well as the other person(s) involved.

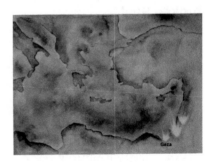
Gaza

- Consider how Philip's approach and witness can help us as Jesus' disciples now.

> *Let Egypt come with gifts of precious metals;*
> *let Ethiopia bow in submission to God.*
> *Sing to God, you kingdoms of the earth.*
> *Sing praises to the Lord.*[33]

---

[33] Psalm 68:31-32, NLT

Day 21 Acts 9:1-19a — Damascus

Should we be surprised when God does something totally unexpected? Probably not, but we are! Only God could have foreseen Saul's conversion. Neither the believers in Jerusalem who had suffered at Saul's hands (8:3, 9:1-2 & 26) nor the Christian community in Syrian Damascus (135 miles NNE of Jerusalem) could ever have imagined this astonishing transformation. Saul's conversion is referenced three times in Acts (see also chapters 22 & 26), an indication of its huge importance.

The living Lord and the broken Saul

"Why are you persecuting me?" (v4). Was he? So closely bound is the Lord Jesus to his people that to persecute them is to persecute him: see Luke 10:16. Saul is struck down and overwhelmed by the instant, seismic revelation of the glory of Jesus. The foundations of his life collapse under him, and he is left powerless, isolated, and fearful. The combination of "Lord" and "Jesus" (v5) demonstrates that Jesus of Nazareth is the Lord of glory. How could Saul have been so badly, horribly wrong? This proud, zealous, fundamentalist Pharisee is left utterly helpless,

groping in the darkness and dependent on others for assistance. He goes three days without sight, following his post-resurrection encounter with Jesus. The old Saul is dying, so a new person can emerge from the gloom into which he has been plunged. We can scarcely imagine all that was happening within Saul as those days passed; one comment offers hope, when the Lord says: "he is praying" (v11).

"Yes, Lord…but, Lord…"

To Ananias is given the task of going to pray for Saul and welcome him into the family of God. Would you have gone, especially given the circumstances (v13-14)? However scared, Ananias goes to Judas' house on Straight Street (still there today) where the church's number one earthly enemy is lodging. Laying his hands upon him, he prays for him, and utters these amazing words: "brother Saul"!

The scales fall from Saul's eyes. He can see again. He is filled with the Holy Spirit. After being baptised, food is served and shared, the most wonderful fellowship meal Saul has ever experienced, and his strength returns.

Amazing grace! How sweet the sound
that saved a wretch like me
I once was lost, but now am found,
was blind, but now I see. [34]

The late Rev. Jim Graham once remarked that when God calls us to be baptised, he invites us to attend our own funeral! The old Saul had to die before the new Saul could be born. See 2 Corinthians 5:17. Saul will later speak powerfully of baptism as union with Jesus in his death and resurrection: see Romans 6:1-11. At this point in his story, it's the wonder of it all that impacts his life. He is a new man, a new creation, united to Jesus, and with a new family. God makes all things new!

Going further...

• Ananias' information about Saul is accurate, but outdated. Do we ever prejudge others without taking into account the possibility of God being at work in them? Don't! But do pray expectantly, and be obedient to God's call.

• Three descriptions of Christians are found in this story — followers of "the Way" (v2), "saints" (v13), and "all who call on your name" (v14). What do these tell us about those early believers? How would you like to be known today?

• Look at the map of this area. Note how the church has moved north to Samaria, west and south to the coast (Acts 8), and now north east to Syria. Give thanks for the unquenchable fire of God spreading across the world today.

---

[34] John Newton (1725-1807)

Day 22 Acts 9:19b-31

Luke's great interests lie in the spread of the gospel of the kingdom and the growth of the church. Fitting a clear timeline into his account can be tricky. The notes below are one plausible explanation of the particular period referred to in today's passage.

Damascus: Persecutor to Preacher

The persecutor is welcomed by those he had previously targeted. The atmosphere is electrifying. Now the persecutor becomes a preacher; Saul is being totally transformed by God. From Galatians 1:15-17 we learn that he left Damascus and spent most of the next 3 years in Arabia before returning to the city. Back in Damascus the preacher is persecuted by those who now oppose him. Under the threat to his life from the governor, he is unceremoniously removed by his new followers lowering him in a basket by night down the city walls. See 2 Corinthians 11:32-33.

Jerusalem: via Stephen, Ananias and Barnabas

When Saul subsequently travels to Jerusalem, his reception is decidedly cool. The disciples there remember him, and don't believe he has truly changed! Step forward Barnabas, "son of encouragement." Luke tells us in Acts how God used three men in significant ways in Saul's life. The prayer of Stephen as he died (8:1), the obedience of Ananias when God spoke (9:17), and the encouragement of Barnabas in Jerusalem, were all of huge significance in the life, experience and spiritual development of Saul, who would become the greatest missionary the world has ever known.

Saul's stay in Jerusalem is invaluable, as he spends time with Peter and James. See Galatians 1:18-24 and 2:9. What did they talk about? Perhaps the life, words and deeds of Jesus? What a time that must have been. James, the Lord's previously unbelieving brother, and Saul, the previous persecutor of the church, are united in devotion to Jesus and his mission in the world. The resurrected Lord has impacted their lives completely and permanently.

Further threats to Saul's life lead to him being removed to Caesarea, then on to his home town of Tarsus; we hear nothing more of him for 10 years, until Acts 11:25-26. Meanwhile, under the encouragement of the Holy Spirit, the church continues to flourish, as Luke tells us in his latest summary. "These summaries function like triumphant choral refrains in the book, as they ring out with joy over what God is doing."[35]

Going further...

• "Now I am happy all the day" is a line from an old hymn celebrating conversion. Is it accurate? Sometimes, as with Saul, conversion signals the start of troubles, not their end. How then can we best support new believers?

• Thank God for those whom he has used in your life. Pray for those you in turn can support and encourage as they follow Jesus. A Bible class leader in late 15th. century Germany used to welcome the young people in his group by standing at the door as they filed in, removing his hat as a token of respect for them, wondering how God might work through them. One of that group was a boy called Martin Luther, whom God would use in such an amazing way in the Protestant Reformation.

---

[35] Bock, page 372.

Day 23 Acts 9:32-43

The healing of Aeneas

As the unquenchable fire spreads, Luke's focus now shifts from Saul to Peter. His travelling ministry takes him to Lydda, Sharon and Joppa (check these eastern Palestinian locations in your Bible maps). In Lydda, God uses Peter to heal Aeneas, a paralysed man, bedridden for eight years. The authority to heal has been bestowed upon Peter and the other apostles by Jesus (Luke 9:1, 6 & 10:9). Aeneas' healing heralds a significant spiritual harvest. There are occasions like this when God works powerfully through the transformation of one individual, whose life has a great impact on the community.

The raising of Tabitha

In the Mediterranean coastal town of Joppa (modern Jaffa), the wonderful story is told of how the disciple Tabitha (or Dorcas) is raised from death. Peter's actions are patterned on the practice and leading of Jesus; Peter had been present when the Lord himself raised individuals from the dead, in Matthew 9:25, Luke 7:11-17, Luke 8:51-56 and John 11:1-44.

In all these Biblical stories of dead people being brought back to life, there is no record of them sharing their experiences beyond death, nor is there any interest in that. What matters is God's power over death, now decisively overcome through the death and resurrection of the Lord Jesus.

We should avoid being sucked into speculation arising from contemporary accounts of near death or beyond death experiences; far better to concentrate on Jesus' victory, and the eternal life he offers. Don't probe unnecessarily where Scripture doesn't go. Rejoice rather in the impact of the gospel through transformed lives like Aeneas and Tabitha (v35 &42).

Apostolic lodgings

Luke's passing comment that Peter lodged in Joppa with Simon, a leatherworker, or tanner, is very interesting. Usually such tradespeople lived somewhat apart from the rest of the community. Why? Because of the Jewish fear of ritual contamination through contact with dead animals; and also (perhaps more practically) because of the smells from their work and tanning processes! There is no special treatment for the apostles.

Peter is happy to associate with a lowly working man, just like his Master Jesus.

Lord of eternity
dwells in humanity,
kneels in humility
and washes our feet...[36]

Going further...

• Can you think of one significant conversion you know of that brought much spiritual fruit? Share that story in your group, and pray for more like it.

• Sadly many televangelists have reputations for high living and luxurious lifestyles: quite a contrast with Peter's B&B arrangements (v43)! "Be willing to associate with people of low position" — Romans 12:16. What might that mean for you?

---

[36] Graham Kendrick, © Meekness and majesty, 1986 Kingsway's Thankyou Music.

Day 24 Acts 10:1-33 — Caesarea

In Acts we see the rapid spread of the gospel throughout the ancient Middle East. Ethnic and national divisions are overcome as God gathers his people; one particular division has to be decisively faced. The separation and antagonism of Jews and Gentiles runs like a religious fault line through this story. Is the gospel for all, or just for the people of Israel? The story of Peter and Cornelius brings this tension into the open in an unforgettable way. Daniel Bock says this is the turning point in Acts; from here the gospel will fan out in all directions. Reverberations will be huge for the life of the church, it's future growth and spread.

In the world of the New Testament, the great divide was between Jews and Gentiles. Ephesians 2:11-12 vividly captures the reality of the *dividing wall of hostility*

(Ephesians 2:14) between these two groups. Howard Marshall says this was the decisive issue in the story of the early church. How then could, and can, the vision of Jesus in Acts 1:8 be realised? Acts 10 leads us into the answer, through two further visions…

Cornelius and his vision: v1-8
What a good man Cornelius is. From the outside you would probably say he was a fine Christian — God-fearing, devout, generous to others in need, someone who prays regularly, a good husband, father, boss…and a Gentile Roman army officer. He doesn't yet know Jesus, nor what God has done through him, but he is on the way. Although "acceptable" to God (v35), his faith is incomplete.

Later, when Peter arrives and speaks, note how central Jesus is in all he says (v34-43). For the present, how encouraging to note that when people genuinely seek after God, he delights to meet with them. In the case of Cornelius, God speaks to him through an angelic vision. Trusted servants are called as Cornelius recounts his story, and then dispatches them to find and invite Peter to come.

Peter and his vision: v9-23

Meanwhile, hungry Peter has a very different vision. As a loyal Jew, he would observe all the dietary requirements that went with obedience to the law. The notion of killing and eating unclean animals is anathema to him; yet, in his trance, this is what God tells him to do three times. "Surely not, Lord" (v14) is a contradiction: if he is Lord, obedience is compulsory.

Uncertain what the vision means, Peter hears words of assurance from the Spirit when Cornelius' servants come looking for him. God is at work in Cornelius, and in Peter; the implications of how God moves in this story will be immense for this loyal Jewish

apostle and his future ministry. So Peter will soon set off for Caesarea with six believers from Joppa (Acts 11:12). It's only a 30 mile journey, but spiritually and theologically Peter's journey is of cosmic proportions.

The two visionaries meet: v24-33

At first it's an awkward meeting. No doubt Peter feels uncomfortable, entering a Gentile environment where, as a Jew, immediately he will be technically unclean; and Cornelius is unsure how to greet his honoured visitor. The large gathering in his home suggests that Cornelius has many friends who, like him, are spiritually seeking, and intensely expectant as Peter enters the room.

Going further...

- V33b provides a wonderful depiction of how any congregation should be as God's word is opened and shared. It's also a humbling verse for any preacher to consider. Pray for your congregation and for those who share God's word regularly.

- What divisions do you perceive that need to be challenged by the gospel? What can you do to address these?

God is working his purpose out as year succeeds to year.
God is working his purpose out, and the time is drawing near;
Nearer and nearer draws the time, the time that shall surely be,
When the earth shall be filled with the glory of God
as the waters cover the sea.[37]

---

[37] A. C. Ainger (1841-1919)

Day 25 Acts 10:34-48

Witness

Try and put yourself into Peter's shoes. You've had a thrice-repeated vision, a communication from God, then a considerable journey, and are now faced with a room full of Gentiles, all eagerly waiting to hear what you have to say. As you begin to explain what God has done through Jesus, perhaps you're wondering what will happen next. Then, to your amazement, God directly intervenes, in a way that finally convinces you this is indeed all legitimate, a gathering orchestrated by God, directed and blessed by the coming of the Holy Spirit…yes, even upon these gathered Gentiles!

It's like a second Pentecost. Cornelius and his friends experience mass conversion. They receive the Holy Spirit and begin speaking in other tongues, extolling God. There's no doubt whatsoever that this is truly a move of the Spirit, and Peter is clear that these new believers should be baptised in the name of Jesus Christ.

Welcome

Many books have been written about Acts 10, because it is perceived to be so significant in the early story and development of the church. The greatest division of Jews/Gentiles is dramatically overcome by the gospel of the kingdom of God, the work and power of the Holy Spirit.

There will be one church, and that church will be the new community, the new society, built and established by Jesus himself. There will be challenges to this, as the unfolding story will reveal, but the principle has been powerfully laid down, that the gospel is for all who will call upon the Lord, just as Peter had stated on the day of Pentecost itself, quoting from the Old Testament prophet Joel (Acts 2:21).

One indication of the drastic change in Peter's outlook is the implied acceptance of the invitation to stay with these new believers for some days (v48). This would almost certainly involve eating food previously regarded by Peter and his Jewish companions as not kosher. Uncircumcised Gentile believers join with Jewish believers sharing in Christian fellowship and hospitality.

"If God had welcomed the Gentiles, it only remained for

the church to do so. Baptism had become the outward sign of reception into the people of God."[38] A seismic change in Peter's experience, understanding and outlook had taken place. The repercussions for the future of the church would be huge.

Going further...

• Read Acts 2:21 again. Peter correctly quoted from Joel, although he was yet to see the implications of that truth, and of the earlier anticipation in the covenant promise to Abraham extending to "all the families of the earth" (Genesis 12:3). Ask God to reveal the implications of grasping and living out his Word of truth today.

• Whenever Peter is asked to speak in Acts, he focusses on Jesus. Note the key points he makes in his sermon in v34-43. What can you learn from Peter for times when you have opportunity to share the good news?

Different faces, different races,
He made us one —
Jesus taught us how to live in harmony[39]

---

[38] Howard Marshall, commentary on Luke.

[39] Graham Kendrick, © 1986 Kingsway's Thankyou Music

Day 26 Acts 11:1-18

Dealing with conflict?

If you thought the previous few days have been over-emphasising the division between Jews and Gentiles, this passage makes it abundantly clear. Peter's return to Jerusalem ignites a disagreement with circumcised, Jewish believers critical of his association (involving fellowship and food) with uncircumcised Gentiles. You can imagine this being replicated throughout the Judaean churches as news spreads about what happened in Caesarea. There is conflict.

There will always be some conflict in the life of the church, so don't be surprised when it arises. The real question is how we deal with it. There are good guidelines in this passage…

* Share what God has done: v4-17

That's where Peter starts. His experience of the vision in Joppa and the visit to Cornelius in Caesarea is communicated accurately, substantiated by the six companions who had gone with him.

* Listen with open minds: v18

Often we enter conflict with minds already made up: bad idea. We need to listen carefully to what others say, seeking to discern in their words how God has been working, and wants to work in us.

* Keep focussed on Jesus: v16-17.

"No further objections" (v18, NIV) sounds like a lawyer's courtroom statement. It captures acceptance of what God is doing, and results in praise, even as these Jewish believers face the challenge of living in a new reality. "God has granted **even** the Gentiles repentance into life". The coming of the Spirit upon these Gentile believers highlights the fact that the Holy Spirit "is the fundamental sign of the new era and of God's activity."[40]

* Be sensitive to others

Apparently Gentiles did not need to become Jews, nor Jews Gentiles. Distinctions often need to be made between what is core to the gospel message, and what is more cultural in our practices.

---

[40] Bock, page 404.

Going further...

- Pastors and leaders who feel threatened and defensive when criticised, be encouraged. Even the apostle Peter faced criticism. V3 could be paraphrased — "You went in and ate with Gentiles, so what about it? Explain yourself!" So what can we learn from Peter's response?

- What conflict(s), if any, are you facing right now? How can the principles expressed above be transferred into contemporary issues? How should we pray as we seek to handle these situations in a way that honours the Lord?

> *Watch o'er Thy Church, O Lord, in mercy,*
> *Save it from evil, guard it still,*
> *Perfect it in Thy love, unite it.*
> *Cleansed and conformed unto Thy will.*
> *As grain, once scattered on the hillsides,*
> *Was in the broken bread made one,*
> *So from all lands Thy Church be gathered*
> *Into Thy kingdom by Thy Son.*[41]

---

[41] From the Didache, 2nd. century, versified by F. Bland Tucker, 1895-1984.

Day 27 Acts 11:19-30 — Antioch (Syria)

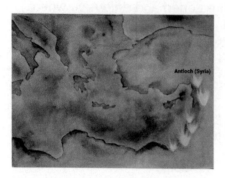

The unquenchable fire spreads rapidly. Luke's latest summary incorporates the impact of the previously recorded persecution following Stephen's death. The good news is spread north-east, across the Mediterranean Sea to the island of Cyprus, and 300 miles north overland to Antioch, capital of the Roman province of Syria. After Rome and Alexandria, Antioch was the third city of the Roman empire, with a population around 300,000—600,000.

Who planted the Antioch church? Not the apostles, but unknown disciples, pioneers who carried and shared the good news of the gospel. Initially comprised of Jewish believers, the arrival of some disciples from Cyprus and Cyrene resulted in a great number of Gentile converts believing and turning to the Lord. Growth continued when Barnabas, sent from the Jerusalem church, arrived and began ministering there. After going off to search for Saul, Barnabas brought him to Antioch, where they ministered together for a year. In Antioch the word "Christian" is first applied to the believers: it may have been a term of reproach but clearly designates those belonging to Christ. What a story; what a church...

* Antioch: the first predominantly Gentile congregation.
Barnabas' role there mattered immensely. He's the only person Luke describes as "good" (v24). His recognition of God's work in Antioch, his encouragement of the disciples there, and his awareness to seek and bring Saul to help, all contributed to the effectiveness and growth of this strategic church.

* Antioch: the church that first received the name "Christian."
Was this a nickname given in ridicule of these people who were always talking about Christ? It seems to have been

used by others and not by Christians themselves; it only recurs in Acts 26:28 and 1 Peter 4:16.

* Antioch: the birthplace of Christian foreign missions (Acts 13:1).

The formation of a church at Antioch would be of great importance in the missionary expansion of the church. Jerusalem may have been the mother church; yet Antioch became the church that grasped the mission heart of God.

* Antioch: where prophecy and care went together.

v27-30 tell us of a visit from a Jerusalem prophet, Agabus. His prediction of a coming famine led to immediate action as the disciples collected money to send to their Christian family members in Judea. Why Judea? Was the need greater there than elsewhere in the Roman world, in part because of the earlier sale of property and land to provide for poorer brothers and sisters? See Acts 2:44-45 and 4:32-37. Whatever the reason, the giving was both spontaneous and generous, with donations conveyed to the Jerusalem elders via Barnabas and Saul.

Going further...

• What connotations does "Christian" carry today? How would you like to be known?

• Why do you think it was so important for Barnabas to go looking for Saul and take him back to Antioch?

• Agabus' prophetic ministry inspired the Antioch church to support their brothers and sisters in Judea; one church came to the aid of another. Is there another church your church could help? What support might be appropriate?

*You have called us out of darkness to declare Your praise;
we exalt You and enthrone You, glorify Your name.
We are a chosen people, a royal priesthood,
a holy nation, belonging to God.*[42]

---

[42] David Halden, © 1981 Word's Spirit of Praise Music/CopyCare

Day 28 Acts 12:1-19a

The martyr and the miracle: v1-10

Today your thoughts will almost certainly focus on the wonderful, and humorous, story of Peter's release from prison, and subsequent reunion with the church gathered in Mary's home to pray.

We must also face the sadness and the mystery of the first apostle to be executed — James, the brother of John. Herod's persecution leads to this young man being martyred; and it raises questions we probably won't ever be able to answer. Why is James put to death, and Peter miraculously rescued from prison? How can one apostle suffer and the other be spared? Is God just?

Faith calls us, requires us to live with unanswerable questions, trusting and resting in the God who can be trusted with our lives, and our deaths. If we today live comparatively safe lives, we ought never to forget brothers and sisters who are even now suffering for Jesus, with some of them likely to become present-day martyrs.

Jesus predicted that James and John would "drink from my cup" (Matthew 20:23). James was martyred and John was persecuted and exiled. Pray for their modern day counterparts.

The praying church: v11-19

Peter's miraculous deliverance from prison (probably in the condemned cell), through the presence and power of an angel, seems at first like a vision or dream. Set free, and having come to his senses, he heads for the house where he knows many will be gathered. The servant girl Rhoda is so overcome with excitement on hearing Peter's voice outside the door that she rushes back to announce he's there, only to be met with incredulity and disbelief.

What had the church been praying for Peter? His safety and release perhaps, or was that too much to expect? Now, at the last moment, God has answered in a direct, dramatic way — and they can't believe it, declaring that poor Rhoda is out of her mind, or perhaps Peter's angel is at the door.

Meanwhile Peter keeps on knocking. The angel has opened the prison doors to set

Peter free, but the church is unwilling to open its door and let him in!

"When the church prays, the cause of God will go forward, and his enemies will come to naught, even if this does not exempt the church from martyrdom and suffering."[43]

Going further...

• Brothers James and John had become followers of Jesus at the same time, and were part of his inner circle of three apostles. Now James has been put to death, and Peter imprisoned. How would John feel? What would you say to him?

• What do we expect when we pray?

May the shadow of Thy presence around our camp be spread;
Baptise us with the courage with which Thou blessed our dead;
O keep us in the pathway their saintly feet have trod;
For the might of Thine arm we bless Thee, our God, our fathers'
God.[44]

---

[43] Howard Marshall, commentary on Luke

[44] C. Silvester Horne (1865-1914), *For the might of Thine arm we bless Thee*

Day 29 Acts 12:19b-25

Herod's blasphemy and God's judgement

One of our most sacred obligations is to offer worship; but to whom? Believers in all ages have no doubt — the Father God revealed in his only Son the Lord Jesus Christ, who comes to us as the Holy Spirit. This is the only true, triune God.

To offer worship to man-made gods or human beings deprives the living God of the worship that is truly and uniquely his. That's why idolatry is so consistently and roundly condemned in scripture, and why today's reading makes for sobering reflection. The tyrannical ruler Herod may have received his due reward for his bloodthirsty regime; yet underlying God's judgement upon him is Herod's willingness to accept worship that belongs only to God.

Herod's grandfather was the Herod who ordered the execution of babies around Bethlehem when Jesus was born. The brutal and bloodthirsty reputation of the Herods continued under his grandson's regime, whose latest round of ordered executions (v19) reinforces that terrible reputation. Soldiers perceived as having failed in their duty are given the same sentence as the escaped prisoner. Sadly, such tyrants as Herod appear frequently throughout human history. These words are being written as Vladimir Putin's troops lay waste to Ukraine, while the rest of the world looks on in horror and revulsion. "Power tends to corrupt, and absolute power corrupts absolutely."[45]

Herod's story is a reminder that all tyrants, indeed all of us, will one day face the judgement of God. In Herod's case it comes hard on the heels of the meeting with representatives from Tyre and Sidon, on the Mediterranean coast (modern day Lebanon).

Conscious of Herod's power economically and strategically to control supplies of food and commerce, they come to petition him. Trying to end their quarrel and appease Herod's anger, the people's delegation respond to his address with words of worship and acclamation: "this is the voice

---

[45] Lord Acton (1834-1902), in a letter written to Roman Catholic Bishop Creighton in 1887.

of a god, not of a man." And immediately God's judgement falls, with Herod struck down by an angel of the Lord and suffering a gruesome death, probably some days later.

Meanwhile, "the word of the Lord continued to increase" (v24). We may face perplexing issues about tyrants who seem to rule unopposed, and whose empires prosper and expand. Many Psalms (eg. 73) lament this apparent inconsistency; yet the writers come to the conclusion that the Lord reigns; ultimately what matters is that his word endures and flourishes.

Crowns and thrones may perish,
kingdoms rise and wane,
But the Church of Jesus
constant shall remain:
Gates of hell can never
'gainst that Church prevail;
We have Christ's own promise,
and that cannot fail.[46]

Going further...

• There are three main characters in this chapter — James, Peter and Herod. With your group, think about how God works in different ways with different people. How is he working with you?

• How can we prepare to face Judgement Day? Should it make us afraid, or filled with hope?

• In spite of all the persecution and threats, the church continues to pray faithfully and, as God blesses it, to increase (v24). Pray for continuing increase in God's church today.

---

[46] Sabine Baring-Gould (1834-1924), *Onward Christian soldiers.*

Day 30 Acts 13:1-3

From stories featuring Peter, Luke moves now to the ministry of Barnabas and Saul. They had been given the task of taking the money collected from the churches at Antioch (and other places) for famine relief to the believers in Jerusalem and Judea (Acts 11:27-30). Now they have returned to Antioch (12:25).

It's there that one of the most significant moments in the history of the early church takes place, a pivotal point in terms of God's mission in the world. This predominantly Gentile church becomes the springboard for the fulfilment of Jesus' vision in Acts 1:8, as the Holy Spirit speaks into the gathered community who are worshipping the Lord and fasting. The church planted in Antioch takes up God's call, rather than the mother church in Jerusalem.

Previous expansion had been triggered by persecution (11:19-20). Now the church makes a decision, inspired by the Holy Spirit, that will result in churches being established in Cyprus, Galatia, Philippi, Thessalonica, Corinth, Ephesus, and many other places. Check out these locations on a map: all emerging from this congregation responding to the voice of God. A number of notable features of this church stand out; for example…

* **Shared leadership**: dig a bit deeper to appreciate how this plurality of leaders represents a mixed group racially, socially and ethnically, yet bound together in Jesus.

* **Openness to God**: initially dependent on Barnabas and Saul, others had emerged from within the congregation whose gifts are recognised and used ("prophets and teachers," v1). Any distinction between their respective gifts seems to be slight, with mutual acceptance and sharing.

Everett F. Harrison suggests "the teacher provided basic information for living the Christian life; the prophet furnished special guidance from the Lord as needed."[47]

* **Earnest endeavour:** fasting and praying appears to be one way of these people demonstrating their commitment to the Lord, and

---

[47] Harrison, *Acts - the expanding church*, page 202

their eagerness to be guided by him.

* **Obedience:** once they hear from the Holy Spirit, after further fasting and praying they send off Barnabas and Saul, probably at the time the two most outstanding leaders in that congregation.

Obedience requires the church not only to let them go, but commission them to go. They gladly give their best people for the mission of God, and entrust them to the guidance and empowering of the Holy Spirit.

Going further...

• "The Holy Spirit said..." although we don't know exactly how it was said, or through whom it was spoken. How does the Holy Spirit speak to us today? How can we guard against spurious claims to divine guidance, yet simultaneously, and more importantly, keep ourselves open to discern when he speaks?

• What is the significance for this church of fasting and praying (v2 &3)? Should we fast and pray today? If so, why and when? How can we maintain the benefits without succumbing to the ostentatious fasting condemned by Jesus (Matthew 6:16-18)?

• How do you think the Jerusalem church felt when God used the Antioch church to initiate such major mission expansion?

> *Speak, O Lord, as we come to You*
> *To receive the food of your holy word.*
> *Take Your truth, plant it deep in us;*
> *Shape and fashion us in Your likeness,*
> *That the light of Christ might be seen today*
> *In our acts of love and our deeds of faith.*
> *Speak, O Lord, and fulfil in us*
> *All Your purposes, for Your glory.*[48]

---

[48]Stuart Townend & Keith Getty Copyright © 2005 Thankyou Music

Day 31 Acts 13:4-12 — Cyprus

Having a good map of the New Testament world is a great asset in following the unfolding story in Acts, especially as the first specific missionary journey gets underway. Initially we head for Barnabas' homeland in Cyprus, nowadays a holiday island that will be familiar to many.

As their journey begins, there are some questions I would like to ask Barnabas and Saul…

Q: "How did you know where to go first?"
All Luke tells us is that the Holy Spirit led the Antioch church to "set apart for me Barnabas and Saul for the work to which I have called them" (v2). They head out dependent on the Holy Spirit to lead them where they should go, and sometimes (later) where they should avoid, even if only for a time.

How dependent are we on the Holy Spirit, and how do we learn to discern his voice?

Q: "Why did you often start preaching in Jewish synagogues?"
Was their understanding that Jews with a grasp of the Old Testament would be best placed to consider the good news about Jesus? Or that being in a context of worship and teaching was conducive to sharing the good news? Certainly the style of preaching reflected in many passages (e.g. Salamis today, and Pisidian Antioch in tomorrow's reading) builds on some Biblical knowledge.

In our day, when there is scant awareness of Biblical stories, where should we start when sharing the good news?

Q: "What persuaded Saul to pronounce temporary judgement on Elymas?"
It's a scary moment, a power encounter, used by God for the proconsul's conversion, and a sobering manifestation of the kingdom of God. Such dramatic meetings underline the Lord's supremacy and authority over all the powers of the evil one.

Q: "Why does 'Saul' change to 'Paul' from now onwards?"

Was 'Saul' more Jewish, and 'Paul' more suited to travel in Gentile regions? Paul now appears to be the key figure as "Barnabas and Saul" becomes "Paul and Barnabas."

I wonder how Barnabas felt about that? Good mentoring enables those who are mentored to flourish, even if that means they go way beyond their mentors in serving God. Would Barnabas rejoice in Paul's emergence and effectiveness? What do you think?

"Barnabas was able to share the stage with Paul and eventually trained him to be able to step ahead. Good leadership can often be measured by whether it leaves a trail of successors behind it. Barnabas not only encouraged Paul; he also enabled him. Barnabas did not feel the need to be always the front man."[49]

Going further...

• First go back and think about the questions already posed.

• Read v12 again noting the phrase "he was amazed at the teaching about the Lord." The miracle of Elymas' temporary blindness impacts the proconsul, yet it's the word/teaching that is decisive.

• Elymas the Jew rejects the message, while the Gentile Sergius Paulus responds. How might this affect us as we share the good news?

---

[49] Bock, page 467.

Day 32 Acts 13:13-43 — Antioch (Pisidia)

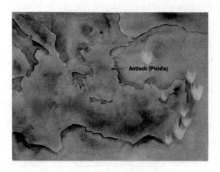

Antioch[50], part of the Roman province of Galatia, a further 100 miles inland, across the Taurus mountains.

Synagogue worship at the time consisted of reciting the creed, prescribed prayers, reading of the Law and Prophets, and an address by any competent person. Paul certainly qualified, given his strong Jewish credentials, upbringing and education.

His message builds on the Old Testament story of the exodus and the later development of the monarchy, culminating in God's inspired prophetic fulfilment when Jesus appears, heralded by John the Baptist.

Perga and separation

We're off once more on a Mediterranean journey, 140 miles north west to Perga, in modern-day Turkey. Here John Mark leaves the missionary group. No reason is given; this departure will lead to open tension between Paul and Barnabas. Could their later separation (15:36-41) have been avoided if they had faced the issue at the time?

We can only speculate, yet flag up how important it is, if there are tensions amongst Christian leaders, to deal with them as soon as possible.

Jesus is the promised Saviour (v23, a title only found in Acts here and in 5:31), risen Lord (v30), God's Son (v33) and Holy One (v35). Through God's action in Jesus, forgiveness of sins is offered by faith, with all who respond being justified by God.

Pisidian Antioch and God's Promise

Without John Mark's help, the mission nevertheless continues in the synagogue at Pisidian

The response is significant (v43) with many apparently

---

[50] There were 16 Antiochs, established by Seleucus Nikator to honour his father Antiochus.

displaying signs of the grace of God at work, keen to learn more about God's promises fulfilled in Jesus.

The pivotal person of Jesus

Paul's use of Old Testament quotations are all relevant to the person and work of Christ. How much there was in the Old Testament anticipating him; how could they have missed the clues liberally sprinkled all through the scriptures they knew so well?

He is not only the one predicted millennia before, but the very pivot of redemption history. The Old Testament anticipates him, and the New Testament unfolds the wonder of who he is. Have you missed him? Thank God there is still time.

God's saints of old through history told
Of the One who was to come:
A son, a king, a Lamb to be slain
for the sins of all the world.
He's the promise of the Ages, lifted up to save us,
Jesus Christ, our Sacrifice.
He's the Fount of living water, King and Friend forever,
Bow before the Promise of the Ages.[51]

Going further...

• Are there any situations you face right now where actions have led to disagreements, as happened when John Mark left the team (v13)? What can you do to help resolve these? Why does it matter so much?

• There are numerous Old Testament references to the coming of Jesus; yet these devout Jews couldn't see. Ask God to open your eyes to the truths revealed in scripture, visible to those with eyes to see, enlightened by the Holy Spirit.

---

[51] Ed Cash, Keith Getty & Stuart Townend Copyright © 2014 Alletrop Music, Getty Music Publishing (BMI), Townend Songs

Day 33 Acts 13:44-52

The aftermath of that memorable day in the synagogue reads like a revival story. The following Sabbath (a week on from v43) almost the whole city gathers to hear God's word.

How wonderful — or is it? Revival stories often record strong opposition; in this case it emanates from the Jews, jealous of how people are responding to Paul and Barnabas.

The word of the Lord

"The word of the Lord" (or of God) is mentioned 4 times in this short passage — v44, 46, 48, and 49. The phrase encapsulates the preached message, the received word in the Old Testament, the good news that evokes thanksgiving, and the power of the gospel unleashed throughout the region.

It was Jeremiah who once described God's word being like a fire burning within him.[52] God's powerful ministry through Paul and Barnabas is spreading that fire exponentially throughout the Middle East. And wherever it spreads, there will always be some who try to extinguish it. Once again Paul, Barnabas and their group face persecution, stirred up by the jealous Jewish leaders, inciting (believe it or not) "the God-fearing women of high standing and the leading men of the city" (v50).

People may be God-fearing yet gospel-resistant. We have noted already how times of revival have often been opposed, not least by other Christians, uneasy with what is going on, and perhaps secretly jealous (see v 45) of the way God is blessing? Here is a salutary warning for us to avoid rushing to judgement when we see or hear of apparent moves of God with which we might be uncomfortable.

Salvation to the ends of the earth

Almost certainly, the attraction of Gentiles to the word of the Lord through Paul and Barnabas was a major influence in the Jewish opposition.

Yet, as the Old testament quotation from Isaiah 49:6

---

[52] See Jeremiah 20:9, and 5:14

74

shows (v47), God's missional intention all along was that through his Servant-Messiah his word of salvation would be for Jews and Gentiles alike, and would reach to the ends of the earth. Isaiah saw it and said it (as did many others in the Old Testament) yet the Jewish people generally rejected it, as they did Paul and Barnabas, who symbolically shake the dust from their feet as they are forced out of town (v51).

Pray that we won't miss something God has clearly said in his word because of our preconceived ideas of what we think it says, or want it to say.

Going further...

- Paul's normal strategy in evangelism was to reach out to the Jews first (eg 14:1), then the Gentiles; almost invariably, the latter group was more responsive. In your situation, is there a particular group either resistant to the gospel, or open to embrace it? How should we pray as we evangelise today?

- Persecution may bring strong rejection and expulsion, yet, paradoxically, it can also result in disciples being "filled with joy and with the Holy Spirit" (v52). How on earth does that work?!

Day 34 Acts 14:1-20 — Iconium, Lystra & Derbe

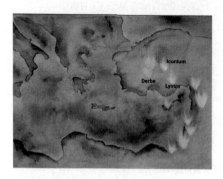

The places identified in this passage will be included in the general letter sent by Paul "to the churches in Galatia" (Galatians 1:2). 2 Timothy 3:11 also makes reference to the problems Paul experienced in this region. With Barnabas, he is travelling the well-known commercial Roman road known as the Royal Road, and they reach the high plateau city of Iconium at 3,370 feet above sea level, now in central Turkey.

Who would be an apostle?
V4 &14 are the only places Luke refers to Paul and Barnabas as apostles. 2 Corinthians 6:3-10 gives a very personal Pauline account of some of the sufferings endured as apostles. Here in Iconium (around 60 miles south east of Pisidian Antioch) there is opposition as opponents try to poison people's minds against

accepting God's word. Paul and Barnabas face a plot to be beaten up and stoned, and opt to move on.

In Lystra, 18 miles south, they are used by God to bring healing to a man lame from birth, the first public miracle associated with Paul. This event initially brings great acclaim, verging on deification, and the crowd prepares to worship the apostles. Part of the problem may have arisen from the fact that in excitement the crowd starts to speak in their own language (v11), unknown to Paul and Barnabas. As the apostles realise what is happening they act to stop such blasphemous behaviour.

Some time later (between v18 &19) the mood turns nasty when troublemaking visitors arrive from previous ministry locations, and use their persuasive powers against the evangelists. The mob turns on Paul, who is stoned, and left for dead.

He recovers and moves on to Derbe, a further 35 miles southeast. This incident and its brief telling can easily obscure the deep shock, pain and discomfort, as Paul continues painfully on to another city. Have any of us ever been stoned?

What apostleship really means

Sometimes people aspire to positions of leadership and authority, often with a strong inner desire for prestige and power. Conversely, in these true-life dramas Luke presents, we see true apostleship. Death threats, physical violence, false accusations, bitter opposition, sudden departures, all are woven into the fabric of New Testament apostleship, and will be the experience of some followers of Jesus in every age. "We must go through many hardships to enter the kingdom of God" (v22).

Is it worth it? What kept them going, and what keeps us going when things get really tough, painful, and terrifying? The answer? Jesus.

All I once held dear, built my life upon
All this world reveres, and wars to own
All I once thought gain I have counted loss
Spent and worthless now, compared to this

Knowing you, Jesus
Knowing you, there is no greater thing
You're my all, you're the best
You're my joy, my righteousness
And I love you, Lord[53]

Going further...

• Idolatry is a powerful force against embracing the gospel. What shape or form does idolatry take today? How should we handle it?

• The phrase "servant leader" has come to be associated with the distinctive ethos of leadership exhibited and commended by Jesus. What aspects of that kind of leadership do you see in Paul and Barnabas? Pray for your leaders.

---

[53] Graham Kendrick, © 1993 Make Way Music

Day 35 Acts 14:21-28

Fruitful Derbe

Derbe proves to be a fruitful sphere of ministry, with "a large number of disciples" won (v21), and apparently no opposition — a welcome relief! Only one sentence conveys what must have been a considerable input of time, prayer, preaching and teaching.

Luke's summaries often belie the effort involved by the apostles, yet also capture the wonderful blessing of God upon their hard work.

Strengthening believers

On occasions the apostles get away from hostile communities, yet bravely go back to strengthen those they have left behind, and encourage them to go on as they follow Jesus.

The appointment of elders (v23) is seen as a key aspect of ensuring good pastoral care and feeding of the flock. The emphasis on prayer and fasting underlines the spiritual significance of the role of the elders appointed. And the warning about hardships (v22) maintains realism regarding the Christian life; it's never easy, but it leads into the kingdom of God.

Back to Antioch

Perhaps up to 2 years after the initial visits, they return via previous locations, taking the long road back. They make their way back to Syrian Antioch, where this first missionary journey had started. There they report what God has done as they travelled, sent out in obedience to the Holy Spirit's direction to this church.

One of the key features of this report is the recognition of how, through their ministry, God has opened "the door of faith to the Gentiles" (v27). The implications of this will be felt forever after in the story of the Christian church.

Going further...

- As you think about the words from the hymn below[54], take some time to reflect, and give thanks, for God's work in your

---

[54] Arthur Campbell Ainger (1841-1919), *God is working his purpose out*, verse 3.

church and community, and perhaps through those you support in other parts of the world. Rejoice in the spread of the gospel, and the advance of the kingdom of God. What open doors do you see now (v27)?

• What are the key roles of elders (or those who fulfil similar tasks perhaps with different titles)? What can we learn from this passage about how they are appointed?

From utmost east to utmost
west
wherever man has trod,
by the mouth of many
messengers
rings out the voice of God:
listen to me, you continents,
you islands, look to me,
that the earth may be filled
with the glory of God,
as the waters cover the sea

Day 36 Acts 15:1-21

Many writers see this chapter as the central point in Acts. One author says: "If the Jewish-Christian extremists had succeeded in imposing their views on the Church…it would have led to two churches, Jewish Christians and Gentile Christians…more probably, it would have meant the end of Gentile Christianity."[55]

The problem: v1-4
Look back to Acts 14:27, and Luke's emphatic note about Gentiles entering the church. But **how** should they come into the church? That's the question that arises in chapter 15, an issue that threatens the very life of this young church.

It all kicks off in Antioch with some visitors from Judea. Their view? If you want to be saved, you've got to be circumcised: effectively, you need to become like a Jew in order to become a Christian. The ensuing debate results in a delegation, headed by Paul and Barnabas, being sent to Jerusalem for a consultation with the apostles and elders there. Often in the history of the church similar questions have been asked. So listen carefully to what emerges from what has become known as the Council of Jerusalem, and how their decision is reached.

The discussion: v5-18

* **Listen** to Peter, whose previous experience years before with Cornelius (Acts 10) feeds directly into this issue. What matters is those whom God accepts by grace through faith in the work of Jesus (v11), sealed by the Holy Spirit (v8).

* **Listen** to Barnabas and Paul, as they recount their stories of God at work in power evangelism amongst the Gentiles.

* **Listen** to James, who in turn finds prophetic endorsement of Gentiles coming to the God of Israel, in the words of Amos 9:11-12 and Isaiah 45:21-25. God's new people, from every race, are to be found in the church.

* **Listen! Listen to God!**
Sometimes we need to be silent (v12), so we can really listen to what God has said, what God has done, and is doing. That leads us towards

---

[55] William Neil, New Century Bible Commentary on Acts.

discernment. Yet when we feel strongly about something, we want to plead our case and win the argument.

Be still. Stop talking. Listen.

The decision: v19-21

James takes the lead in proposing a compromise to be conveyed from this gathering, on the basis that, "It seemed good to the Holy Spirit and to us" (v28). The compromise respects those who struggle with heathen worship, together with those from a Jewish background whose principles are strong but not core to the gospel, and it stresses the need for holiness in life and sexual ethics.

Crucially, for Jews and Gentiles alike, apart from the response of faith to the grace of God through the Lord Jesus (v11), nothing additional is needed in order to be saved. As long as there is no compromise on the gospel, diversity of expression can be tolerated.

Going further...

• As you think about this Jerusalem gathering, consider how hard it is for us to adopt radically new ways of thinking. What are some of the concerns we face today that require us to grapple with the gospel and apply it?

• Galatians 5:1 (possibly written before or around this time) aptly expresses the resounding conclusion of the Jerusalem council. What does it mean for us to have freedom in Christ?

Thy hand, O God, has guided
Thy flock, from age to age;
the wondrous tale is written,
full clear on every page;
our fathers owned Thy goodness,
and we their deeds record;
and both of this bear witness:
One Church, one faith, one Lord.[56]

---

[56] Edward Hayes Plumptre (1821-91)

Day 37 Acts 15:22-35

Sharing the news

Can you imagine the disciples at Antioch waiting nervously for the decision reached in Jerusalem? When the letter arrives, personally delivered by leaders they know well, accompanied by some from the mother church, there is great joy. There is no question that these Gentiles believers are genuine and accepted by God; there is also exhortation for a fourfold abstention:

(1) **From food sacrificed to idols:** this was commonplace in a world where pagan temples and wayside shrines seemed to be everywhere. Food sold in the markets had often been ceremonially offered to pagan gods before appearing on the stalls.

(2) **From blood, and**
(3) **from the meat of strangled animals:** both of these were forbidden in Jewish law, so Gentiles are being asked to accept limitations that show respect for other believers who come from a different background.

(4) **From sexual immorality:** pagan temples often housed cult prostitutes. Such behaviour associated with pagan worship could easily permeate society and have a negative impact on moral standards.

Far from appearing limiting and dictatorial, the Gentile believers in Antioch rejoice when they hear the letter, and its tone. God-given wisdom fed into the hearts and minds of those who composed this epistle, in a way that affirmed the Antioch Christians.

The blessing

The outcome of the Jerusalem church gathering seems entirely positive, unless you are firmly entrenched in a legalistic position.

The subsequent building up of the Antioch church underlines how unity invokes the blessing of God: see Psalm 133. Barnabas and Paul are joined by Judas and Silas, representatives from Jerusalem, all involved, with many others (v35) in encouraging, strengthening, teaching and preaching the word of the Lord.

Going further...

- Dietary restrictions on a religious basis (v29) may seem far removed from us today. By contrast, sexual immorality is blatant and widespread. What should govern our behaviour as God's people in the 21st. century?

- How many people in the church should be involved in preaching and teaching? Is there room in your congregation for many voices to share in building up God's people? How can that work best?

Day 38 Acts 15:36-16:5

When Christians disagree…

What happens when things go wrong? When Christians disagree and separate? When decisions are made against that backdrop? And why does it happen?

Luke doesn't answer all these questions, but gives an honest record of what took place here. Bible writers consistently paint realistic pictures of the "heroes" of the faith.

They are sinful people, just like us, and subject to the same weaknesses and failures. The painful separation of what had been a fruitful partnership must have been felt acutely by both Barnabas and Paul.

Who was right and who was wrong? Should Paul have agreed with Barnabas and accepted that John Mark's previous departure from their group could be forgiven? Or was Paul right to stress the need for commitment and dependability from those charged with missionary endeavour?

As Barnabas and John Mark leave for Cyprus, Paul and Silas go in the opposite direction. Luke's focus stays on Paul, who is commended by the church, which suggests the believers supported him in the dispute. Sometimes we just have to live with the consequences of our actions, although we should do everything possible to work towards reconciliation.

Yet God is still sovereign. Even out of debate and disagreement he can still bring blessing if we genuinely offer ourselves in service to him. Cyprus will benefit from the further visit of Barnabas and Mark, while Paul and Silas form a new partnership that will bring significant growth and blessing in Syria and Cilicia, and lead to the recruitment of a new member to the team, a young man called Timothy.

Dear Lord and Father of mankind
Forgive our foolish ways.
Reclothe us in our rightful mind,
In purer lives thy service find
In deeper reverence, praise,

in deeper reverence, praise[57]

Teenager Timothy

Paul's invitation to Timothy, probably a teenager at this time, to join the team, would prove immensely important.

Although often in the background, more is known about Timothy than most of the apostles. After Jesus, Peter and Paul, he is the most frequently mentioned character in the New Testament. Almost certainly he had heard Paul preach in Lystra, and may well have been present when Paul was stoned.

Following Timothy's circumcision, apparently carried out to obviate any problems with Jewish acceptance of him, he is fully involved in the mission to communicate the decision from Jerusalem, and build up the churches.

Going further...

• Paul and Barnabas would not see each other for some time following this separation. How do you think they coped, as they wondered what they did and said, and whether the whole situation could have been handled differently? How could they work towards reconciliation? What can you do if you are faced with a similar breach in fellowship?

• Timothy is an example of a young person becoming fully involved in apostolic mission and ministry. What encouragement and opportunities do we give to young disciples today? How can we foster their growth and development?

---

[57] John Greenleaf Whittier (1807-82)

Philippi

Day 39 Acts 16:6-15 — Philippi

When God says "no"!
This passage is fascinating. Twice in quick succession the Holy Spirit prevents planned action. Neither Asia nor Bithynia are to be visited yet; their time will come.

We don't know how the Holy Spirit made this clear to Paul and his team, nor why, but there seems no doubt in their minds. And perhaps while they are mulling this over, the Macedonian vision received by Paul convinces them of the direction they are to take.

Until this point in Acts, Dr. Luke has been recording events based on the information he has carefully gleaned from others. Now Luke himself joins Paul and his companions on their journeys, and so begins to speak consistently in the first person plural. "When Paul had seen the vision, immediately **WE** sought to go on into Macedonia" (v10). Having relied on the testimony of others, Luke is now himself an eyewitness of all that will follow.

Philippi

Responding to the Macedonian call leads them to Philippi, in present day Greece. The businesswoman Lydia from Thyatira, a dealer in popular purple cloth, becomes the first convert in Philippi, soon joined by her household. Her home becomes a place of hospitality for Paul, his companions, and likely for the church that will emerge.

Philippi will become a special place for Paul. His later letter to the church there (Philippians) is perhaps his warmest, most joyful epistle, expressing something of the place these people occupied in his heart.

Over the years I have heard many calls for strategic church planning, mission statements, vision casting, goal setting, etc. These may be useful, yet they can also be a distraction from earnestly seeking the guidance of the Holy Spirit, who may well take us in a different direction from what we had envisaged.

Obedience to God sometimes means declining what seems to us to be the obvious or best course of action. We need to make sure that whatever plans we make are derived from the Spirit of God, and subject to his sovereign control. The Acts story is about letting God be God, and learning his ways in fulfilling the prophetic mission of Jesus in Acts 1:8.

Going further...

- How do we keep in step with the Holy Spirit? What leads us in his way, and how can we guard against mistaken or spurious claims to inspiration?

- If you were charged with planting a church, where would you start, and who would you like to respond to Christ first? Look again at how Paul, Silas, Luke, Timothy and the others went about this in Philippi, in today's and tomorrow's readings; what can we learn from them?

Day 40 Acts 16:16-40

"My chains fell off"
Charles Wesley wrote these famous words in one of his timeless hymns, reputedly following visits to prisons to share the good news. Wesley was speaking about the wonder of conversion, being set free from sin through the sacrifice of our Lord Jesus Christ on the cross.

Wesley's inner experience was quite literally the experience of Paul and Silas in that Philippi prison. Their incarceration follows the deliverance of the demonised slave girl and the consequent riot that provoked. Why? Because her "owners" (v19: what a terrible word, carefully chosen by Luke) see their business prospects plummet as her fortune-telling abilities cease, and they stir up a supportive mob.

Paul and Silas endure a severe flogging and are thrown into jail, secured in the stocks, bleeding and battered, with nothing done to ease their painful wounds. Their response? "About midnight Paul and Silas were praying and singing hymns to God" (v25).

How incredible is this! Yet in God's mysterious economy it follows on supernaturally from the words of Jesus in Matthew 5:11-12. It is replicated today across the world where persecuted believers find a strange supernatural ability to rejoice even in their suffering.

Like the late Richard Wurmbrandt who endured years of solitary confinement, imprisoned by the ruling Rumanian communist regime; one night, so overwhelmed was he by the sense of the presence of God, that in the darkness and squalor of his cell he got up and danced with joy.

"My heart was free"
The shocked prison jailer, like the prisoners, is not only stunned by the praise and prayers, but shaken to the core when an earthquake hits Philippi. The prison doors swing open, and the prisoners' chains fall to the ground. Suicide seems the best way out, knowing what punishment awaits. Maybe an even bigger shock is when he hears Paul's restraining voice, just as the jailer prepares to fall on his sword. The prisoners have not escaped!

This man's deep, heartfelt question (v30) is perhaps the most important question that anyone can ever ask.

"I rose, went forth, and followed thee"

Turn back to the second bullet point in the *"Going further…"* section yesterday. We now have the assembled people who comprise the first church members in Philippi. There's the businesswoman Lydia, her household, probably the slave girl, the jailer and his family. Would you have chosen such a motley crew to begin a church in this Macedonian (now Greek) city? Time to read 1 Corinthians 1:26-31.

Going further...

- So as you look at your church, what do you see? A motley crew? A strange assortment of people, not many you might have picked as your dream team to get the church going? Or do you see those God has chosen — sinful, simple, vulnerable, weak, foolish, humble; yet men, women, teenagers and children who have found in Christ all that they are not? Now they, with you, are the body of Christ on earth! If that doesn't make you want to give thanks and praise God, I don't know what will.

Day 41 Acts 17:1-15 — Thessalonica & Berea

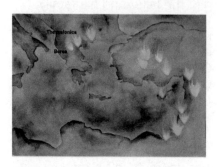

What's the difference between the Macedonian capital Thessalonica (100 miles from Philippi) and Berea? Apart from the obvious factors like distance (about 50 miles), geographical location, population, industry, and so on. Why does the Jewish constituency in Thessalonica, with some exceptions, resist the message Paul brings, while many Jews in Berea believe the word of God? Most of the converts there are not Jews but Gentiles (v4).

In Thessalonica the people who react violently against Paul **think** they know what the Scriptures say. In Berea, the people **want** to know what the Scriptures say. There's a great gulf between these two positions.

Jewish opposition is nothing new for Paul. Proclaiming

Jesus as Messiah is divisive; you either believe it or you don't. If, as a devout Jew, you don't, then it is blasphemous to affirm Jesus in this way, and to offer prayer to him. Yet when Paul teaches about the nature of the Messiah's role and identity, he consistently uses the Old Testament Scriptures over three successive weeks in Thessalonica (v2-3).

These religious people **think** they know what the Scriptures say, so if they are right, there can be no argument. Anything or anyone who threatens their position is rejected.

Berea is so different. Again the Jewish community is the first group to receive the message. Their predominant response is open-minded, to examine what the Scriptures actually say; they **want** to know the truth, and respond accordingly. Perhaps that influences the decision to leave Silas and Timothy at Berea for a time, to minister there, while the endangered Paul is sent off to the coast.

Do you **think** you know what the Scriptures say? Do you

want to know? John Robinson was an early 17th. century English Nonconformist church pastor, who moved across the North Sea to Holland in the search for greater freedom to worship. In 1620 many of his congregation were preparing to sail back to England, and then onward to America with the Pilgrim Fathers on the ship Mayflower.

An eyewitness, Edward Winslow, described the scene and the message Robinson gave to his departing flock:

"He charged us, before God and His blessed angels, to follow him no further then he followed Christ; and if God should reveal anything to us by any other instrument of His to be as ready to receive it as ever we were to receive any truth by his ministry. For he was very confident that the Lord had more truth and light yet to break forth out of His holy word."[58]

The hymn-writer George Rawson (1807-89) used these famous words when he penned his hymn —

We limit not the truth of God
To our poor reach of mind,
By notions of our day and sect,
Crude, partial, and confined;
No, let a new and better hope
Within our hearts be stirred:
The Lord hath yet more light and truth
To break forth from His word.

Going further...

• Can you recall a time when your understanding of the Scriptures was challenged and changed? How did you feel, and what persuaded you to take a different view? Are there situations you face now where you need to step back from a strong, dogmatic position, and take time to dig deeper into the Bible for guidance?

• What aspects of the Bereans' approach to Paul's message do you find encouraging? How can you and your group/church replicate these, seeking God's light and truth?

---

[58] Quoted in the Baptist Hymn Book Companion, page 217.

Day 42 Acts 17:16-33 — Athens

Lonely in Athens
Having been sent away from Berea, and having experienced the value of being part of a close-knit team, Paul now finds himself without some of his trusted friends in Athens. Silas and Timothy had been sent instructions to come as soon as possible.

We sometimes have unrealistic images of the people we regard as heroes of the faith. This is one of those moments when we begin to grasp how emotionally demanding apostolic ministry can be. Yet Paul presses on, with an inner compulsion to make Jesus known, even in multi-cultural, multi-religious Athens.

The unknown God
Luke's description of Athens may be slightly tongue-in-cheek (v21), but nevertheless conveys an accurate sense of the ethos of this Greek capital city, steeped in cultural history that still influences our world. In the midst of a plethora of altars and idols, one stands out and provides Paul with an opportunity to preach.

Although "greatly distressed" by the widespread idolatry he sees throughout the city, note too how Paul actively but graciously confronts the Athenians, meeting them where they are spiritually. He neither condemns them, nor condones their idolatry.

Message and tone are important in sharing the good news, whether that be in synagogue, city square, or philosophical debate. "Too many Christians know their own message but understand far too little about how and why others think as they do… whether in informal conversation or in formal settings, the ability to set forth the faith at a level appropriate to the setting is a valuable talent."[59] Don Richardson offers a fascinating account of how the altar[60] "to an unknown god" possibly came to be there, perhaps from six centuries earlier.[61] The same author, in his initial book *Peace-child,* introduces us to the idea of redemptive analogy: that is, in every culture God has already provided a key (redemptive analogy) for the people of that culture to begin to grasp the gospel. The task of a missionary herald, guided by the Holy Spirit, is to identify that key and use it to open the door to an understanding of the good news that allows people to respond to Jesus. Athens offers one example of that process. Following debate, discussion, and proclamation, the result is that most are curious, some mock, and some believe (v32-34).

Going further...

- There are some converts in Athens, although not the large numbers Paul had experienced elsewhere. Why do you think that was so?

- Verse 21 suggests that to many Athenian thinkers, discussing ideas was more valuable than pursuing truth. What can we learn from Paul about communicating the gospel today in a culture where just about everything seems relative, and many shun the notion of absolute truth?

- How do you respond to the statement that Jesus will be our Judge (v31), as well as Saviour and Lord?

O for a closer walk with God, a calm and heavenly frame,
a light to shine upon the road that leads me to the Lamb...
...the dearest idol I have known, whate'er that idol be,
help me to tear it from Thy throne, and worship only Thee[62]

---

59 Bock, page 573.

60 Or altars, with some suggesting there were many like this scattered around the Areopagus.

61 Don Richardson, *Eternity in Their Hearts*, chapter 1, Regal Books.

62 William Cowper (1731-1800)

Day 43 Acts 18:1-17 — Corinth

Fears, edicts and friends
Moving on to Corinth, a commercial centre and a city with a reputation for immorality, 50 miles due west of Athens, Paul later records his anxiety and fear at the challenge ahead: see 1 Corinthians 2:3. Given the city's reputation, not many of us would have chosen to live there.

Mercifully, and providentially, he meets with Aquila and Priscilla, a couple first mentioned here, who will become stalwarts in the early church. Forced out of Rome by edict of the emperor (v2), they offer encouragement and support to Paul. God can work through the edicts of emperors to help his servants in need, and to establish congregations in the toughest of places.

Preaching Christ in Corinth
Joined by Silas and Timothy, arriving from Macedonia, Paul devotes himself to preaching, released from his income-generating work as a tentmaker (v3). Initially ministering in the synagogue, the general rejection of his message by the Jews leads him to preach among the Gentiles; although some notable conversions amongst the Jewish community are recorded (v8).

It may be that during this time, Paul travelled wider than Corinth itself, as 2 Corinthians 1:1 suggests. And thanks to these later letters sent to the church at Corinth, we have a good summary of his message and approach in that city. See 1 Corinthians 2:1-5.

Paul's night-time vision, and the consequent, uninterrupted 18 month period of work in Corinth, must have been a great relief after so much opposition elsewhere. Such periods seldom lasted for Paul, although the latest opposition from a Jewish quarter backfires when the Roman proconsul Gallio[63] dismisses their complaint, sending it back for them to resolve themselves (v15-16).

Poor Sosthenes[64] becomes a focal point for anger, frustration, and violence; although it's not clear if this is

---

[63] Gallio was proconsul in Corinth AD51-52.

[64] See 1 Corinthians 1:1, perhaps the same Sosthenes mentioned here.

perpetrated by the Jews, or the Greeks venting their feelings against the Jews.

Corinth and Ephesus

"Corinth and Ephesus were the two most important cities visited by Paul in the course of his missionary work, and he stayed in each for a considerable period in order to establish churches which would then evangelise the surrounding areas."[65] Howard Marshall's comment reminds us that the church does not exist for itself, but for active participation in the mission of God.

In God's plan, churches make disciples of Jesus who plant other churches who make disciples of Jesus, and so on. "I will build my church"[66] says Jesus.

Give thanks for the church to which you belong; it's not perfect, but it's there, and it belongs to Jesus. Nothing can stop the unquenchable fire of God. Let it burn within us today.

Build Your Church, Lord,
make us strong, Lord,
join our hearts, Lord, through Your Son,
make us one, Lord, in Your body,
in the kingdom of Your Son.[67]

Going further...

• Paul had seen the Lord Jesus at his conversion; now he encounters him in a vision (v9-10). How have you met with Jesus? Give thanks as you share something of your story with others.

• We've read a number of times now of Christians suffering violence because of their allegiance to Christ. How can we support brothers and sisters going through such trials?

---

[65] Marshall, Acts.

[66] Matthew 16:18

[67] Dave Richards, *For I'm building a people of power*, © 1977 Kingsway's Thankyou Music.

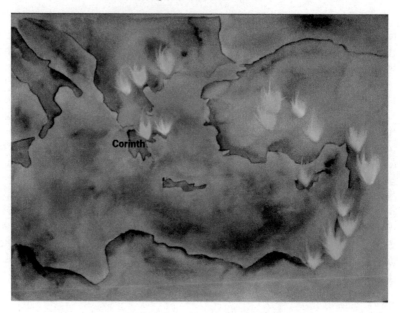

Day 44 Acts 18:18-28

Back to Antioch, via Ephesus
Luke's story throughout Acts is carefully told, and his historical information specifically arranged. Paul's few weeks in Athens (chapter 17) receives roughly the same length of treatment as his 18 month ministry in Corinth. Like a master painter Luke selects the images that will contribute to his overall depiction of how the fire is spreading, under the guidance and inspiration of the Holy Spirit.

And after each Pauline period of outreach, preaching, teaching, and church planting, the church at Antioch is revisited as the base from which this has all developed.

When did you last go back to the church you consider your spiritual home? Maybe a return visit would bring great encouragement. En route to Antioch, Paul visits Ephesus briefly, with the hope of coming back later for longer. He also leaves Priscilla and Aquila there. From now on when this couple are mentioned, Priscilla is usually first[68]; this may denote her

---

[68] See v26, also Romans 16:3 and 2 Timothy 4:19.

higher social standing, or her more prominent leadership role.

What about Paul's vow and head shaving (v18)? This may have been a temporary Nazirite vow (see Numbers 6:1-21), or a private vow to express thanks to God for his faithfulness and provision (see v9-10), customarily ending with the head being shaved.

Time in Antioch is precious, yet the needs of the new churches demand ongoing involvement and support, so a third missionary journey begins for Paul. His itinerary takes him first to Galatia and Phrygia to strengthen the disciples. One verse (23) covers a round trip of approximately 1500 miles, presumably mostly on foot. The Proclaimers sing about walking 500 miles for love[69]; how far would we walk for the kingdom?

Priscilla, Aquila and Apollos

Meanwhile, back in Ephesus, we meet Apollos, a deeply spiritual Jew from Alexandria in Egypt, well versed in the Scriptures, an able communicator, fervent in spirit (literally "on fire"), yet with a significant gap in his understanding. It seems he knows little of the finished work of Jesus the Messiah and the coming of the Holy Spirit. A home visit with Priscilla and Aquila proves immensely useful in helping Apollos grasp the gospel more adequately, and equipping him for even more useful future ministry[70]. When they realise what he lacks, Priscilla and Aquila do not deal with him in public, but invite him to their home; they don't impede his ministry, although he has much to learn. Recognising his effectiveness, they encourage him to grow. What a wise couple!

Going further...

- Priscilla and Aquila heard Apollos speak and recognised his need for further instruction. Have you ever been in that position? How did you respond? Are you still open to listen?

- See v26 and 1 Corinthians 16:19. How can you use your home for God?

---

[69] The Proclaimers, *I'm gonna be (500 miles)*, 1988, from the album *Sunshine on Leith.*

[70] Some commentators have suggested Apollos as a possible author of the unattributed book of Hebrews.

Day 45 Acts 19:1-22 — Ephesus

Ephesus alive

By their very calling, apostles are usually nomadic, moving from place to place, preaching the gospel, establishing churches, moving on. As already noted, Paul's longer stays in Corinth and Ephesus break that pattern. The cosmopolitan town of Ephesus, with its estimated 300,000 people, is where Paul spends the longest time in one place, and with good reason.

The encounter with the "incomplete" 12 disciples (v1-7); the openness to minister for three months in the synagogue (v8); followed by the availability of the lecture hall of Tyrannus (v9-10), all indicate an open door of opportunity in Ephesus. There are obvious signs of the powerful activity of the Holy Spirit — he comes upon those 12 disciples; he empowers Paul to perform extraordinary miracles (a telling phrase, since miracles are usually regarded anyway as extraordinary!); he moves among the people in such a way that many previously engaged in sorcery openly confess their evil deeds and burn their scrolls, valued at 50,000 days' wages.

Paul's 2-3 year sojourn in Ephesus may be regarded, humanly speaking, as the most fruitful period of his apostolic ministry. Luke's summary statement (v10) expresses just how the word of the Lord spread through the province of Asia (in present day Turkey).

Were the 12 disciples truly believers prior to Paul's proclamation and prayer? Were the extraordinary miracles intended to be a pattern, or simply a record of what happened? What about the demonic verification of Paul's credentials (v15)? To be used in deliverance ministry, and known by demons, is quite a statement of this apostle's divinely granted authority.

Whatever our questions might be, all these incidents testify to the work of the Holy Spirit. Add the huge bonfire as a further indication of the kingdom of God arriving in Ephesus, a centre for occult activity, and you have a wonderful demonstration of God's power impacting a whole society. To say "the word of the Lord spread widely and grew in power" (v20) almost seems an understatement by Luke.

Letters and lectures

Many of the churches mentioned in Paul's travels later received letters from him. When were these written? Mostly we can only guess; yet it's good, when reading about a particular church and location, to read right through any corresponding New Testament letter. Dating and place of writing may be ultimately uncertain, yet reading them within the context of Paul's travels can be very illuminating. Some may well have been written in Ephesus. Brief mention of Paul's future plans (v21) indicates a burning desire to seek new areas of ministry, right into the heart of the Roman empire.

Some manuscripts suggest Paul used the lecture hall of Tyrannus when it was not needed for normal teaching activities, which usually started early in the cooler part of the day. So Paul may have led his discussions from 11am-4pm, the hottest part of the day (siesta time), when people were resting. When the Holy Spirit is at work, physical discomfort seems unimportant compared to engaging with God's word and power.

Going further...

• Read v18-19 again. What might you need to deal with, decisively, to break from and reject the past in order to follow Jesus? Got any matches?

• Can you think of a particular time of blessing in your church? What made it special, and what can you take from that time to inspire and encourage you as you move forward? Talk about this in your group, and pray through the shared lessons you identify.

• Read Ephesians 1:3-14, one long sentence in Greek, Paul's outpouring of praise and thanks to God for what he has done for his friends in Ephesus...and for us!

Day 46 Acts 19:23-41

Ephesus

What a great place to be a Christian, as the gospel impacts the whole community and fans out into the countryside. What a wonderful place to visit today, with huge parts of the old town excavated and preserved. You can quite literally walk down the main street, past the ruins of wayside shops, houses and shrines, imagining the enraged mob thronging around you, pushing you into the ruins of the 25,000 seat amphitheatre where they gather to demand satisfaction…or at least some do.

Luke's witty description (v32) could describe numerous such events through the centuries. When mob rule takes over, common sense and rational thought disappear, unless you have a wise official like the town clerk (v35) who can subdue the masses, talk them down and send them home.

The Way

That's one of the descriptions applied to Christianity here and in Acts 9:2, 19:9, 22:4, 24:14 & 22. Christian disciples do not stand still. They are actively moving along a path set out by God, with a clear sense of purpose and destiny, joining a great all-age procession of pilgrims on a journey, with their eyes fixed on Jesus.

He is described in Hebrews as the "author and perfecter of our faith" (12:2, NIV). He is the one who declares "I am the way and the truth and the life. No one comes to the Father except through me" (John 14:6 NIV). Such a claim may be as unpalatable to many of our contemporaries as to the devotees of Artemis (or Diana) in Ephesus; that doesn't alter the truth of Jesus' amazing statement, nor the pilgrims' journey.

Politics, religion, and the economy

What caused the riot? Genuine concern for the honour of the "great Artemis" (v35), whose massive temple stood overshadowing Ephesus? Or Demetrius and others seeing their business decline sharply as the gospel leads people to turn away from idolatry to the living God? When Christ appears to threaten the economy, people will rise up against him, his message, and his messengers.

Unable it seems to locate Paul (being protected by the disciples and some friendly civic leaders), the mob's fury is directed against Gaius and Aristarchus. Ironically the ringleader Demetrius witnesses to just how widely the good news has spread, when he comments "you see and hear that not only in Ephesus but *in almost all of Asia* this Paul has persuaded and turned away a great many people" (v26, ESV).

Going further...

• What causes (or might cause) people today to rise up against the Christian church and the gospel? How should we respond when opposition becomes blatant and aggressive?

• Isaiah 44:9-23 gives a vivid depiction of the pervasiveness, and stupidity, of worshipping idols. Why do people create and worship idols? What idols are we tempted to follow and worship — money, sex, power? Graham Kendrick says it well...

We call you now to worship Him as Lord of all,
to have no gods before Him, their thrones must fall.[71]

---

[71] Graham Kendrick, *Make way, make way*, © 1986 Kingsway's Thankyou Music.

Day 47 Acts 20:1-12 — Troas

Companions on the journey

Following the riot in Ephesus, Paul moves on to Macedonia and Greece. He is accompanied by seven friends and colleagues (v4), who go on ahead to Troas, awaiting Paul's arrival with Luke. All seven men come from places visited and evangelised during Paul's travels — Berea, Thessalonica, Lystra, and the province of Asia.

Everett F Harrison makes the point that Paul's strategy is "to evangelise…through people he had brought to Christ and trained for service"[72]. If that's accurate, it invites us to ask how much time we give to encourage and train new believers, involving them in mission. Remember also that Timothy was probably a teenager when recruited to join Paul's team.

This practice simultaneously highlights how important it is for people to work together. Effective teams provide mutual support, encouragement, and accountability, and help guard against any personality cult emerging around one particular leader. Effective teams provide an environment in which new leaders can grow and flourish. The Pauline strategic pattern could well be based on the selfsame way Jesus chose, equipped, and commissioned his 12 apostles.

Worship and sleepy disciples

V7-8 are intriguing. This brief depiction reminds us of Christianity being a home-based movement; here believers are gathered in an "upstairs room".

These verses also contain the first reference to Christians meeting not on the traditional Jewish Sabbath (the seventh day, our Saturday) but on the first day, Sunday, renamed as the Lord's Day in Revelation 1:10[73]. Sunday is the day of resurrection, new life and hope for the world through our risen Lord Jesus.

Though it may have been a working day then, for followers of Jesus the significance of meeting on that day, to worship and meet with their Lord, caused them to change a lifelong habit (for those from a

---

[72] Harrison, page 291.

[73] See too 1 Corinthians 16:2

Jewish background). Even if that meant meeting very early before going to work, or gathering later in the day, as here in Troas, meeting on this day really mattered, and was charged with spiritual significance.

An earlier gathering might have suited young[74] Eutychus better! Even listening to the inspiring apostle Paul can send people to sleep, especially if he keeps on talking right through the night (v11). Never complain again about long sermons! Thank God for his mercy to raise Eutychus and restore him to his people.

Going further...

• How do you help new believers, train them, and involve them in the church's life and God's mission? What more can be done?

• The notes above highlight effective teamwork. How is your leadership team functioning? What contributes towards making that team effective?

• In our modern era, we hear many stories about different missional expressions of church emerging, with varied patterns of meeting, sometimes moving away from Sundays. Is there still something important about focussing our shared gatherings on the first day of the week, the Lord's Day, as these early Christians did? If so, it's also worth considering how we can maximise our times together in creative, helpful ways, providing good opportunities to meet and engage with each other and with Jesus. Do our "meetings" always facilitate this? If not, how can they be developed?

---

[74] The word used to describe him suggests he was roughly between 8-14 years old.

Day 48 Acts 20:13-38

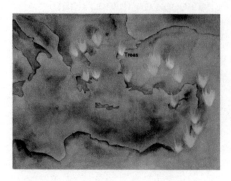

Jerusalem beckons for Paul, as it did for Jesus in Luke's gospel. First there is a deeply moving gathering with the elders of the church at Ephesus, who travel 30 miles south to Miletus for this farewell encounter. Paul's message to them is personal, touching and revealing.

His ministry in Ephesus: v18-21

How can we summarise those 3 years? Authentic, costly, demanding, and fruitful are words that come to mind. Here is an apostle, an evangelist, a pastor, deeply committed to God and the people he has served. He has worked hard to earn his own living (v34); he has faced opposition, hardship and toil; and through it all he has sought to be faithful to his calling, humbly serving the Lord.

His heartfelt desire: v22-24

From his conversion Paul has been aware of his call involving suffering for the sake of Christ[75]. Repeated Spirit-led warnings of what lies ahead (v23) do not dissuade him from heading towards Jerusalem. V24 echoes his later words to Timothy — "I have fought the good fight, I have finished the race, I have kept the faith"[76].

Not many of us will, I guess, have to endure what Paul experienced, yet all of us are called to lifelong discipleship, wherever God takes us and whatever that means. Keep close to Jesus. Keep focussed on him.

His commendation: v25-31

It's particularly poignant if indeed this is the last time Paul will see these beloved friends and colleagues; there may have been a further return to Ephesus later in Paul's life, but at the time this seemed unlikely. These church elders,

---

[75] See Acts 9:16

[76] 2 Timothy 4:7, NIV

or overseers (v28) are charged by Paul...
- To keep watch over themselves
- To keep watch over God's flock
- To be shepherds of the church of God
- To guard God's people against false teachers who will lead many astray

Darrell Bock helpfully comments — "One of the highest priorities for Paul in ministry is that his people will be equipped theologically and spiritually to persevere after he is gone...the Pauline legacy, to ensure that he leaves behind not a monument to himself, but Christians who are a monument to God in their faithfulness."[77]

His confidence: v32-35

God is able to keep them by his grace, to build them up and prepare them for their inheritance in Christ. Paul quotes from Jesus, in a saying we only find here but which presumably must have been passed on verbally, to remind these elders of the keynote of service: it's all about giving, not receiving. Jesus said it and showed what it meant. Now they must follow him.

When the farewell comes, it's a very tearful one. From Luke's words we can sense the emotion as the whole group kneels down, prays for each other, and embraces Paul as they say goodbye...yet for believers such farewells are never final!

Going further...

- Whatever your equivalent title is of elders or overseers (or even bishops as in NIV notes on v28), how can Paul's commendation in v25-31 be implemented in church life today? Pray for those in your church who are called by God to this ministry.

> Oh, to know the power of your risen life,
> and to know you in Your sufferings,
> to become like you in Your death, my Lord,
> so with You to live and never die.
> Knowing you Jesus...there is no greater thing[78]

---

77 Bock, page 622.

78 Graham Kendrick, *All I once held dear*, © 1993 Make Way Music

Day 49 Acts 21:1-14

The parting (yesterday's reading) was deeply emotional, reflected in Luke's words "after we had torn ourselves away from them" (v1). Painful, but necessary, if Paul, like Jesus before him[79], had to go on to Jerusalem, where his destiny lay. So the Aegean travelogue is no cruise, but a step by step journey, via Cos, Rhodes, Patara, Phoenicia, and Tyre, always moving closer to Israel.

Speaking God's words

One of God's wonderful gifts is prophecy. Normally the Holy Spirit uses this for "forth-telling," to edify and encourage God's people, by speaking his words into specific situations and building up his people to obey and serve him.

It also at times involves fore-telling, when future events are predicted. Why? Sometimes to assure suffering people of a different time ahead; sometimes to strengthen faith; sometimes to help prepare his people for what is coming. Here we read of disciples who prophesy (v4), Philip's four daughters (v9), and Agabus (v10).

Discerning God's will

Interpreting prophecy can be challenging. Sometimes the prophetic messages are accurate and clear, while the application of them is not, for example in this passage. On more than one occasion, predictions are made about Paul's coming experience in Jerusalem; and several people, including Luke (v12) interpret this as God's warning not to go there. Paul, on the other hand, is in no doubt that he must go to Jerusalem, and face whatever lies ahead.

He never challenges the prophetic messages, or those who deliver them, but disagrees profoundly with how the prophecies are interpreted and applied.

Sometimes we put an interpretation on what God has said that expresses our wishes rather than what God is saying, which we may find distressing or unacceptable. The gift of interpretation must go alongside the gift of prophecy, even if that means for Paul that his future involves suffering and possible death, for which he is ready (v13).

---

[79] See Luke 9:51-53

Going further...

• Compare v4 with Acts 20:22 — the same Spirit who compels Paul to go to Jerusalem speaks through the disciples at Tyre, who urge Paul not to go. How do you reconcile these two verses, and what lessons can you derive from that?

• Distinguishing what we want God to say from what he does say can be tricky and painful. It forces us to look into our own hearts, to be self-aware and honest. If God's way means suffering, and even death, will we still press on?

*No matter if the way
be sometimes dark,
no matter though the cost
be oft-times great,
He knoweth how
I best shall reach the mark,
the way that leads to Him
must needs be strait.*[80]

---

[80] F Brook, verse 3 of *My Goal is God Himself*, Copyright control.

Day 50 Acts 21:15-36

Arrival in Jerusalem

After their long sea journey across the Aegean and Mediterranean, Paul and his companions arrive in Jerusalem, where they receive a warm welcome from James and the church elders.

Accommodating Jewish scruples: v20-26

The incident Luke records in these verses might seem strange to us. In the context of a sharply divided society, with very strong Jewish sensibilities, Paul's agreement to participate in this ceremony of purification shows graciousness and a submissive spirit. It simultaneously allows him to address false rumours about his attitude to the law and Jewish customs. Paul is a loyal Jew, and outreach to Gentiles is not anti-Jewish. He agrees to the suggestion of the church elders.

Why put unnecessary stumbling blocks in front of his own people, when the truth of the gospel is not being compromised? Why not accept the guidance of the Jerusalem church, as Paul does? In doing so, he lays down principles that will be explained further in passages like Romans 14:1-15:4. His example invites us to consider situations when we need to be accommodating to others in order to preserve unity, and distinguish these situations from cases where truth is threatened.

In essentials Unity,
in non-essentials Liberty,
in all things Charity[81]

Stirring up mob anger: v27-36

Ironically, the elders' request and Paul's compliance lead to trouble in the temple, stirred up by some dissident Asian Jews who recognise Paul and accuse him of anti-Jewish actions and sacrilegious behaviour in the temple precincts. Gentiles could enter the outer court of the temple in Jerusalem, but were forbidden, on pain of death, to go into the inner temple areas.

---

[81] Attributed to the 17th. century German theologian Rupertus Meldenius

The accusations are based on false assumptions (v29) but mobs seldom engage with rational argument. Tempers flare, passions rise, and soon the whole city is disturbed.

Paul is dragged from the temple and violently attacked. Only the intervention of the Roman authorities stops the physical assault on Paul; even then, the crowd is so incensed that the soldiers have to carry Paul to the barracks to take him into custody. The predictions of Agabus and others (v4 & 11) are now coming true. This is the last mention of the Jerusalem temple in Acts, picturing rejection of the one bringing God's message: how sad.

What happens next? Come back tomorrow and find out!

Going further...

• When should we be willing to compromise, and when take an unyielding stand?

• How do you respond when wrongly accused of something? How often have you reached a conclusion based on an assumption (v29), rather than the facts?

• Acts contains frequent references to the inclusiveness of the Christian church —husbands, wives, children (v5), father and daughters (v9), teenage helpers (Timothy, probably others). How can all ages and stages be included and involved in the life of your church? What more could be done to facilitate this?

Day 51 Acts 21:37-22:29

As we enter the last part of Acts, Luke's focus is on what happens to Paul, and how the Spirit uses that for the unquenchable fire of God to spread to Rome itself, the heart of the empire. The events recorded in these final seven chapters, one quarter of the whole book, are interlinked; the coverage given shows how important this section is, as the ministry to the Gentiles is firmly established as key to God's call to Israel. The unfolding story is neither haphazard nor accidental. God is at work. Events may seem to take unexpected twists and turns, yet behind it all is the Sovereign Lord, fulfilling his plan.

I do not know what lies ahead,
the way I cannot see;
yet one stands near to be my guide,
He'll show the way to me.
I know who holds the future,
and He'll guide me with His hand,
with God things don't just happen,
everything by Him is planned... [82]

Paul's story and defence: 21:37-22:21

The journey begins in Jerusalem as Paul delivers his speech, most likely in Aramaic (the everyday Palestinian language), to a hostile crowd. His own conversion story will be told three times in Acts; each telling includes elements relevant to the context. Paul never forgets how God has intervened in his life, and is ready to share that story when he can; it's relevant and powerful because his experience of God is ongoing, not stuck in the past.

He tells his story in conditions we might never face, where his freedom and his life are at risk. For Paul, properly representing the gospel is more important than any personal considerations. That said, he works within the Roman legal system as he defends himself, yet never looks for any loopholes to allow him to go

---

[82] Alfred B Smith & Eugene Clark © 1947, 1958 Singspiration Music/Brentwood Benson Music Publishing

free. Rome has nothing to fear from Christianity (compare 21:38-39, where he corrects the mistaken impression about his identity). His calm demeanour under stress is in itself a powerful witness to those who hear him.

"One cannot withhold admiration for the apostle in this situation…in chains, bruised and exhausted, half beaten to death, yet anxious to bear a testimony to the milling crowd in the court below."[83]

Paul the prisoner: 22:22-29
Listening to Paul, the crowd are quiet until he reaches the Lord's command to him to go to the Gentiles. Like gunpowder awaiting a spark, the peace is shattered and the crowd ignites in anger, calling for Paul's execution.

Spare a thought for the Roman commander, to whom such vehement reaction must be terribly confusing, especially if he struggles to understand what has been said by Paul in Aramaic. Why such a response? How can he determine the facts of the case? Perhaps seeking the truth under the torture of flogging might be the answer? (Sadly, a procedure well documented by regimes all over the world through the centuries since then.)

The commander's plan is, however, abandoned when the startling news is conveyed to him that Paul is a free-born Roman citizen, unlike the commander himself who has purchased his coveted citizenship at considerable cost. He decides to order the Jewish Sanhedrin, or council, to convene the next day and consider Paul's case.

Going further...

- There are a number of mission agencies working in our world today to help Christians unjustly accused of crimes against the state, or blasphemous violation of strict religious laws. Could you offer some support?

- What would you want to highlight from your own story of how God has been at work in your life? Pray for opportunity this week to share this with someone.

---

[83] Harrison, page 332.

Day 52 Acts 22:30-23:11

Still determined to discover exactly what is going on, the Roman commander Claudius Lysias (named later in 23:26), calls for what is effectively a pre-trial hearing to get at the facts.

Before the Sanhedrin

Paul's continued defence before the Jewish council is short-lived. Does he insult the hight priest (v3)? Or is he reacting to an unjust instruction by the high priest to strike him, contrary to the Jewish law he was charged to uphold?

Whatever the nuances of this incident, Darrell Bock makes the point that Paul consistently holds people in respect when he communicates with them. On this occasion, when he is said to have crossed the line into disrespect, he acknowledges it. In our discussions and debates with others, whether they are supportive or antagonistic, here is a good principle to follow. One Christian speaker and apologist remarked that whenever he is invited to debate with an opponent, usually an atheist, he tries to make a point of befriending that person[84]. Respect and grace are powerful Christian virtues.

Paul's altercation with the hight priest Ananias leads quickly to his statement about being a Pharisee, who believes in the resurrection of the dead. At that point it appears no one listens to Paul's words, since the whole Sanhedrin is split into the two main camps of Pharisees, who believe in a resurrection, and Sadducees, who don't. The confusion of the Roman commander must now be even more perplexing. How can he resolve this intense Jewish debate, with Paul caught up in the mayhem, and the commander having to extract him from the volatile, violent dispute, taking him into custody in the safety of the Roman barracks?

"Take courage!"

There is no record in Paul's story of any actions by the Jerusalem Christians on his behalf. There may well have been representations made of which we are ignorant, yet the strong impression is that, for whatever reasons, Paul is on his own...only he's not on his own! No followers of Jesus are ever on their own, no matter

---

84 Professor John Lennox.

how difficult or fearful their circumstances. The very next night, Paul receives a heavenly visitor: the Lord himself stands beside Paul and speaks words to strengthen and encourage.

Paul's witness will continue, even in Rome, the capital of the empire. How can that possibly happen? We will find out as we read on. Meantime Paul can sleep in peace!

Going further...

- When speaking for Jesus, why is it important to do so with respect and grace?

- Have you ever felt alone, isolated, vulnerable as a Christian? Read v11 again. What did that mean for Paul, and how does it help us when we feel so totally alone? Read, pray, and if you know the tune, sing these wonderful words...

    Nothing shall separate us from the love of God.
    Nothing shall separate us from the love of God.[85]

---

[85] Noel & Tricia Richards ©1989 Kingsway's Thankyou Music

Day 53 Acts 23:12-35

Though I walk in the midst of trouble,
you preserve my life:
you stretch out your hand against the anger of my foes,
with your right hand you save me.
The Lord will fulfil his purpose for me;
your love, O Lord, endures for ever...
...Psalm 138:7-8 (NIV)

Compare Paul's words when he writes to the church at Thessalonica: "The one who calls you is faithful, and he will do it" (1 Thessalonians 5:24).

In today's passage we read about the plot in Jerusalem to kill Paul, its discovery, the warning given by his nephew, and the subsequent dramatic night-time journey to Caesarea. On one level, here is a man facing a death threat, at high risk, totally under the control of the Roman authorities, helpless in these extreme circumstances.

There is a deeper level, however. The unseen God, to whom Paul has entrusted his life and destiny, is overseeing and orchestrating the unfolding events. His life is in God's hands, and God's promise stands firm, that Paul must testify to Jesus in Rome itself. Given Paul's present situation, how can that possibly come about? God is at work, and he will make the way.

Be encouraged as you read this story, and see God at work. In particular, note...

- **The discovery of the plot by 40 would-be assassins: v12-15.** What happens when their plan is thwarted we don't know. Either they starve to death (unlikely!) or their anger dissipates when they realise Paul has been spirited away under nightfall. If a vow was impossible to fulfil, those taking it could be released from it.

- **The actions of Paul's nephew: v16-22.** This is one of the few snippets of information we have about Paul's family; how grateful to have an alert nephew in the right place at the right time to overhear the plotters... God is at work once again.

- **The protection offered by the Roman commander Claudius Lysias: v23-35.** The commander's prompt actions and secret removal of Paul, a Roman citizen, from Jerusalem to Caesarea takes him away from the imminent danger. He is still in custody, and will remain a prisoner throughout the period covered in Acts, but he is safe, and steadily moving in the direction of Rome. Why does the commander take this quick action? No doubt his training, leadership and management skills come into play, yet at the deeper level…God is at work.

Claudius Lysias' letter to Governor Felix is somewhat inaccurate. For example, there's no mention of the command to flog Paul, and the commander only discovers he is a Roman citizen after that command is given, not before (v27). So Claudius Lysias wants to be seen in a good light!

Yet, together with others later in Paul's story, he finds no evidence of anything criminal. In his mind, Paul is innocent. Then why not set him free? Like his Lord before him, the accusations levelled against Paul are unfounded. Yet his life is ultimately not in their hands, but in the higher hands of his heavenly Father. He can be trusted.

Going further…

- "The Lord will fulfil his purpose for me." Trace God's hand at work in your life, fulfilling his purpose; as you look back with praise, consider how he is fulfilling his purpose now.

- Pray for Christians around the world unjustly accused and detained or imprisoned. Thank God for those working to draw attention to their plight, and plead their cause. Once again, consider if and how you could you offer them more support.

Day 54 Acts 24:1-27

On trial in Caesarea

In Caesarea five days later, Paul faces a delegation of his Jerusalem accusers in court. The legal advocate Tertullus speaks for the Sanhedrin, cleverly spending as much time complimenting the governor as presenting his case; probably tongue-in-cheek, since Felix is not well regarded by the Jewish leadership. The charges? Paul is a pest, a political agitator, leader of a seditious movement, and was disruptive in the Jerusalem temple.

The accusations are baseless, as Paul declares when replying, refuting them one by one. He makes a confession of faith, not of guilt. The main instigators of the Jerusalem riot (Acts 21:27-29) are not even present to explain their part in the unrest and Paul's subsequent detention.

Governor Felix seems to acknowledge the weakness of the case against Paul, yet plays for time by adjourning the trial, pending further evidence from the commander Lysias (who never seems to show up!).

Paul and Governor Felix

It's the last section in this chapter that I find most compelling and poignant. You sense that Felix is drawn to what Paul has to say, and yet resists the implications of his message.

Their first personal encounter, away from the court proceedings, sets the tone for their frequent conversations over the next two years. Felix is alarmed as Paul speaks about faith in Jesus Christ, about "righteousness, self-control, and the judgement to come." Felix cuts short their meeting. Why?

Is he convicted, given his own track record of injustice, and his thrice-married status? Does he realise the truths in Paul's words, yet resist their personal application? How often do we do the same — inwardly acknowledging that God is speaking to us, yet putting off what we know is the response we should make? Like Felix, we want to decide when it's convenient for us to respond to God; and maybe, like Felix, we have ulterior motives in delay (v26).

Philip P. Bliss wrote a hymn in 1871 that combines Felix's response here with the later words of Agrippa (Acts 26:28) —

"Almost persuaded" now to believe;
"Almost persuaded" Christ to receive;
Seems now some soul to say,
"Go, Spirit, go Thy way,
Some more convenient day
On Thee I'll call."

Felix departs the story without any indication of that more "convenient" time arriving. How sad that this Roman Governor can talk repeatedly with this amazing apostle Paul, can listen to the gospel being presented and applied, yet apparently without any repentance and change. Don't make the same mistake.

Paul remains in custody at Caesarea, although with some privileges, for two years. On the understanding that Luke is almost certainly a Pauline companion throughout this time, it is suggested by some scholars that he uses this time to do his initial research for his gospel and the book of Acts.

In Caesarea he has access to many eyewitnesses of the events he subsequently records.

Going further...

• As we consider Felix, we might feel uneasy as we think about how we are responding, or failing to respond, to God's word. Pray for grace to hear, repent if necessary, turn to God and welcome the work of his Spirit, whatever that means for us.

• Talk with your group about what we can take from Paul's speech (v10-21) to help us in bearing witness to Jesus?

Day 55 Acts 25:1-22

Paul and Festus: v1-12
Felix has been recalled to Rome, succeeded in Caesarea by Porcius Festus, probably around AD60.

On visiting Jerusalem, Festus is met with renewed Jewish complaints against Paul, accusations not forgotten from two years earlier. Back in Caesarea, when Paul appears before him, Festus, wanting to please the Jews, proposes a trial in Jerusalem, not Caesarea. There is a plot afoot to ambush and kill Paul; this time it's the official plan of the Jewish leaders, not the aim of a zealous group. The scene depicted by Luke pictures Paul surrounded by his adversaries, "like a man doing battle for his life in a ring surrounded by ferocious animals."[86]

Is Festus aware of the danger, yet willing to take that risk if it means that the Paul problem can thereby be resolved? You can imagine how he might think about reporting this back to his superiors… "the prisoner requested a trial in Jerusalem, but was ambushed and killed on the way there by unknown assassins… very sad, but these things happen."

Sensing likely danger if he accedes to the governor's suggestion of a Jerusalem trial, Paul makes his appeal to have his case referred to the emperor Caesar (Nero). As a Roman citizen, he has this right. After a hasty consultation with his advisors, Festus grants his request.

Festus and Agrippa: v13-22
Looking for help in understanding and communicating Paul's case to Caesar Nero, Festus turns to (Herod) Agrippa II, great-grandson of Herod the Great who ruled the region when Jesus was born, and his sister Bernice. (Another sister, Drusilla, was the wife of the previous governor Felix).

The governor seems to think that the issues are entirely related to the Jewish religion, a bit of a mystery to him. He has nothing substantial to write, since he can find nothing criminal in Paul; yet he must say something! So with great pomp and ceremony before many civic dignitaries (v23) Paul is brought before the august company…his chains contrasting sharply with the

---

[86] Harrison, page 365.

resplendent crowd of onlookers.
The charges against Paul are political, yet the evidence is theological. How will he respond?

Going further...

• Is Paul's appeal to Caesar premature (26:32), or God's way to ensure that his faithful apostle will witness in Rome, as predicted (23:11)?

• None of those in authority ever seriously question Paul's innocence, yet none are prepared to set him free, not until after his appeal to Caesar has been granted (26:32). Pray for those detained in oppressive regimes across the world today, perhaps without charge or proper legal representation, and for those with authority over them. May truth prevail, and the gospel flourish through the faithful witness of the people of God.

Day 56 Acts 25:23-26:32

This is Paul's third defence speech, and his fullest declaration of the gospel in such circumstances. Claudius Lysias, Felix, Druscilla, Porcius Festus, Agrippa and Bernice have all now heard Paul state his case. None of them finds any guilt in him, yet he is detained in custody, and, having appealed to Caesar, his course is set.

Today's passage is not really a trial, more of an opportunity by Festus to get something he can send to Rome to explain why Paul is being sent there as a prisoner. Wherever Paul is, he is the same man. Irrespective of status, ethnicity, background or importance, all are treated the same. King Agrippa's two statements are key moments in this passage...

V28: This is either a question or a comment. "Do you think that" could also be "so you think that in such a short time you can persuade me to be a Christian?" Either way, he is evading the real issue, posed by Paul's direct question to him in v27. Agrippa does what all of us can do when we are uncomfortable, sensing that we have been asked something that goes right to our hearts, demanding an honest, heartfelt response. The pious king is suddenly the one being questioned by the prisoner.

The scene concludes without any answer from Agrippa, who now must wrestle with his conscience as he considers Paul's piercing question.

V32: Agrippa's final comment provides us with one of those "what if" moments. What if Paul had not appealed to Caesar? Was he right, or wise, to do so? What if Festus had followed his convictions and released Paul? What if those Asian Jews who accused him of desecrating the Jerusalem temple had withdrawn their false charges? What if...? We could go indefinitely.

Against such unsettling questions, we can say some things with certainty...

- **God is sovereign.** Our choices may be right or wrong, wise or foolish, clearly thought out or misguided. Yet somehow God is able to override and even use what happens, to bring about his intended purpose, for his glory.

- **What God has said, he will do.** Paul will go to Rome and bear witness to Jesus there. How that happens is secondary; Paul's focus, and ours, must be to submit to God's plan willingly and embrace his way, however that is worked out in our lives.

- **"What if" questions ultimately get us nowhere.** God works with us where we are, and leads us on from there. "What would have happened if" is a story we will never be told. The real question? "What is my relationship now with God?"

Going further...

• What are the questions you are asking right now? Can you share them with your group, or trusted friends? How are these issues impacting your relationship with God?

Wherever he may guide me, no want shall turn me back;
my shepherd is beside me, and nothing can I lack.
His wisdom ever waketh, His sight is never dim,
he knows the way He taketh, and I will walk with Him.[87]

---

[87]Anna Laetitia Waring (1823-1910), *In heavenly love abiding*, verse 2.

Day 57 Acts 27:1-26

Paul's appeal to Caesar having been granted, arrangements are made to transport him to Rome, together with a few of his companions, including Dr. Luke, whose record of the voyage and shipwreck makes for a gripping read. It's worth charting this journey on a map of the Mediterranean and Adriatic Seas. Here are some highlights from Luke's fascinating account…

V11: The dismissal of Paul's warning: after all, why should the pilot and ship owner listen to a tent-maker and evangelist when it comes to sea-faring matters? Thankfully, Paul's initial warning of danger and loss of life is superseded by the later angelic message.

v14: Because of the geographical situation, Mediterranean storms can hit suddenly with little warning, and last for a considerable length of time.

V20: Luke's vivid description of such a severe storm reaches the point of complete hopelessness, that feeling that can settle in when it seems nothing is working and doom is imminent.

V21-26: The picture of the despairing crew and passengers puts Paul's next intervention into sharp contrast. "You should have taken my advice…" (v21). How often have we wished that we had taken someone's advice? Yet no matter how we got to where we are, God is still able to work within our circumstances

Following the night-time visit of an angel, Paul predicts that although the ship will be lost, their lives will be saved, and encourages everyone to eat, building up their strength.

It's one thing to indulge in wishful thinking and the hope of rescue; it's quite different when you claim that a heavenly messenger has assured you of deliverance. Paul's apostolic credentials are on the line; has God truly communicated with him? If you were on board, battered and despairing after almost two weeks fighting the storm, how would you react?

Going further...

- The Christian life is never plain sailing (pardon the pun!). Following Jesus doesn't mean we will be spared the storms of life; but we know the presence of God will never leave us, even in the most extreme circumstances. Give thanks for his presence with you in hard times, and pray for those going through storms right now.

Though I feel afraid of territory unknown,
I know that I can say that I do not stand alone.
For Jesus, You have promised Your presence in my heart,
I cannot see the ending, but it's here that I must start...

...What lies across the waves may cause my heart to fear,
Will I survive the day, must I leave what's known and dear?
A ship that's in the harbour is still and safe from harm,
but it was not built to be there, it was made for wind and storm,

And all I know is you have called me, and that I will follow is all I
can say;
I will go where You will send me, and Your fire lights my way. [88]

---

[88] Ian White, © 1996 LittleMistyMusic/Kingsway's Thankyou Music

Day 58 Acts 27:27-44

The drama continues as the sailors sense they are approaching land; that in turn brings new dangers of rocks and shipwreck. The sailors' attempt to flee in a lifeboat by themselves is thwarted.

Once again, just after dawn, Paul encourages everyone to eat, with the assurance of being saved. Can those present ever forget Paul's action, for believers so reminiscent of Jesus, when he takes bread, gives thanks, breaks and eats it? All 276 passengers and crew join in this breakfast meal, before jettisoning anything left over, to lighten the ship.

Spotting a beach, the decision is taken to run the ship aground there, but before this can be done a sandbar is struck and the ship starts breaking up. What about all the prisoners on board? If they escape, the soldiers' lives could well be forfeited. Julius the centurion, who had shown kindness to Paul previously, prevents this from happening. Either swimming or supported by broken pieces of the ship, the miracle happens: everyone on board makes it safely to land. What a story; how thankful we are to God for Luke's breathless, eyewitness account.

God has said — three times — that Paul will stand before Caesar to bear witness to Jesus. God is at work to bring his word to pass.

That doesn't mean freedom from danger, suffering or pain. It does bring reassurance that this ship, far from drifting totally out of control, is guided by God to a safe landing place: a vivid analogy for his children on board the ship. Psalm 107:23-32 depicts just such an experience as these sea-farers have had, ending with the words "Let them give thanks to the Lord for his unfailing love and his wonderful deeds for men."

Going further...

- When you think of how God has worked to bring deliverance from danger or death, what personal stories (or stories from close friends) come to mind? Share one of these with your group, and join in thanksgiving for God's saving power.

- Consider how your story or experience could be used to help others facing danger or death.

Rescue the perishing,
care for the dying,
Snatch them in pity from sin and the grave;
Weep o'er the erring one,
Lift up the fallen,
Tell them of Jesus the mighty to save.[89]

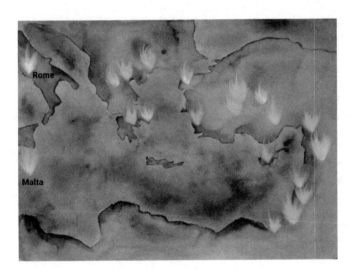

---

[89] Fanny Jane Crosby (1820-1915).

Day 59 Acts 28:1-16 — Malta

Friendship on Malta: v1-10
The dreadful war in Ukraine (begun in 2022) has highlighted once again, in our global community, the plight and the needs of refugees. The Malta shipwreck might seem mild in comparison, yet the "unusual kindness" shown to the 276 bedraggled survivors sets a fine example of how care and friendship can be offered, even to completely unknown foreigners.

Paul's humble example too, the great apostle gathering sticks for the fire, reminds us of the servant heart God looks for in his people. The viper's bite proves harmless, much to the amazement of the local people; the words of Jesus in Mark 16:18 come to mind. God is watching over Paul, protecting him and ensuring once again that his purpose will be fulfilled.

Unexpected blessings come to the people of Malta. Publius' sick father is healed, together with many of the local people who hear the news and come to meet the strangers. Doctor Luke, the physician, appears happy to hold back and let Paul the apostle minister to sick people, perhaps with Luke's support, certainly with wonderful outcomes. Storm and shipwreck result in help and healing; with rest and recuperation for the exhausted travellers.

Fellowship in Rome: v11-16
Three months later, preparations to move on from Malta are greatly helped, once again, by the kindness and provision of the people. A ship is found, landing at last in the Italian port of Puteoli. Some "brothers" are discovered there, who open their homes to Paul, Luke and the others.

"And so we came to Rome" (v15). Luke's understated words belie the great significance of this arrival and final walk to the capital city of the empire. God has kept his word; the new adventure is beginning. Paul is still in custody, but under house arrest (v16).

Meeting someone at the airport or train station can be touching and hugely encouraging. I doubt that many of us would, however, walk 43 miles (to the Forum of Appius) or even around 21 miles (to the Three Taverns) to greet an apostle and his companions! Some will know Paul personally, others will know him only through his letter to the church in Rome, possibly sent a few years earlier. Romans 16 gives a number of personal greetings, and Romans 15:24-29 indicates Paul's desire to visit Rome, en route (as he was then hoping) to Spain.

The reality and warmth of Christian fellowship is a great blessing to Paul, as it is to us, both when it comes from those we know, and from those we have never met, but with whom we feel an immediate bond.

When the writer to Hebrews urges his readers not to forsake gathering together but strengthen and encourage one another[90], he (or she) is aware both of the good and necessary discipline of doing that, and also of the wonderful benefits we receive from time spent together in the Lord's presence. Whatever lines ahead in Rome, Paul is part of the family of God, with brothers and sisters in the capital city.

Going further...perhaps quite literally?

- Practical expressions of care have always been foremost in authentic Christian living. Who is needing help and support around you? How could you assist them?

- At a time when communications were difficult, my late sister Catherine once travelled, alone and unannounced, from Scotland to visit some missionary friends in France, to provide needed support and encouragement. What gesture could you make today, or this week, or soon, to express your agape love for brothers and sisters in Christ?

Blest be the tie that binds
Our hearts in Christian love;
The fellowship of kindred minds
Is like to that above...
...When for awhile we part,
This thought shall soothe our pain,
That we shall still be joined in heart,
and hope to meet again[91]

---

[90] Hebrews 10:24-25

[91] John Fawcett (1740-1817), verses 1 & 4.

Day 60 Acts 28:17-31 — Rome!

Paul and his companions have arrived! The eventful journey to Rome is now behind. The future is unknown, yet the God who has proved faithful can be trusted with what's ahead as well as praised for the past.

Sharing with the Jewish leaders: v17-28

Paul's basic approach continues in Rome as elsewhere. First he reaches out to the Jews, inviting community leaders to come to him since he is under house arrest (v30).

Extensive declaration of the kingdom of God and its fulfilment through Jesus fails to convince most of his hearers, sadly a familiar pattern. Yet they have heard. Isaiah's prophecy, quoted in v26-27, correctly describes their response: hearing but not understanding, seeing but not perceiving.

Why? Because of calloused hearts, bunged up ears, and closed eyes.

Before condemning them, ask how open and receptive you are to God, and how open and receptive we are as communities of disciples committed to Jesus. Pray for tender hearts, sensitive consciences, open minds. God can work with such.

The triumph of the Kingdom: v30-31

Luke's second volume closes with this brief summary of the next two years for Paul and his close companions.

He is under house arrest, yet within that restriction he has freedom to preach the kingdom of God and teach about the Lord Jesus Christ. It is quite likely that during this time, he composes some of the letters to churches previously visited, like Ephesians[92], Philippians[93], Colossians[94], and Philemon[95].

---

[92] See Ephesians 3:1, 4:1 & 6:19-20

[93] See Philippians 1:12-14

[94] See Colossians 4:10 & 18

[95] Philemon 1:1, 8-13 & 22.

On a visit to Crumlin Road Jail in Belfast some years ago, we saw a copy of the late Dr. Ian Paisley's commentary on Romans, written while he was an inmate. Even imprisonment can be a fruitful time.

Why does Luke end his story here? What happened to Paul? Did he die in Rome as a martyr, after facing his accusers before Caesar? Or was he released and able to travel once again, perhaps visiting Spain as he had hoped earlier, only later to be re-arrested, brought back to Rome and suffer martyrdom there? There may be some clues in the pastoral letters (1 & 2 Timothy and Titus); from other sources it does seem possible, even likely, that Paul was released and travelled west, later to face a second, final imprisonment in Rome. We cannot be certain.

When we don't know, we should avoid endless, and ultimately fruitless speculation. Instead we focus on the fact that Acts is not about Peter, James, John, Mary, Philip, Stephen, Priscilla, Aquila, Paul, or countless others. Acts is about the Holy Spirit working to bring about the promise of Jesus who said that he would build his church.

In one generation, the gospel of the kingdom of God has been shared, and the church has been established throughout and in the heart of the Roman empire. There is a church in Rome, the centre of the western world for most of the people alive on earth at that time.

The opening verses of Acts (1:1-3) and these closing verses book-end this second volume of Luke. The kingdom of God has arrived in Jesus, and now is challenging Rome itself. "Boldly and without hindrance" (v31) is described by the late Professor William Barclay[96] as falling like a victor's cry, the peak of Luke's story. The story begun 30 years before in Jerusalem has ended in Rome: a miracle of God.

"God is the hero of Acts, and the plot line is how he reveals his word through Jesus and a faithful church. God will make sure it happens, and so will a faithful church."[97]

The fire of God is unquenchable. Neither persecution, nor political

---

[96] Taken from the Daily Study Bible

[97] Bock, page 760.

opposition, nor demonic activity can extinguish the blaze God has started. It is now for us to carry the torch in our time as we look forward to the return of our Lord Jesus Christ.

We end with the words attributed to William Booth (1829-1912), founder of the Salvation Army, and adapted by Lex Loizides in the hymn *O God of burning, cleansing flame*[98].

To make our weak heart strong
and brave, send the fire!
To live, a dying world to save:
Send the fire today!
O see us on Your altar lay,
we give our lives to You today,
so crown the offering now,
we pray:
send the fire today,
send the fire today.

---

[98] 1994 Kingsway's Thankyou Music.

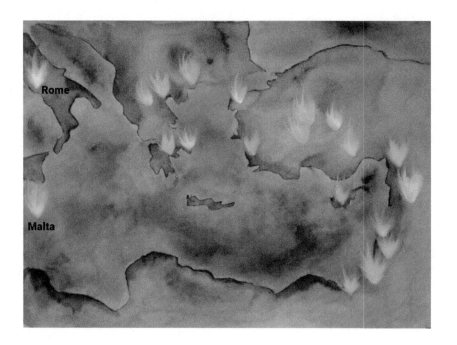

ABOUT THE AUTHOR AND ILLUSTRATOR

John G. Greenshields is a retired Scottish Baptist Minister who has served churches in Shettleston (Glasgow), Leslie (Fife) and Bridge of Don (Aberdeen). His ministry concluded with 8 years working as Ministry Development Coordinator for the Baptist Union of Scotland.

His previous devotional books on Luke's Gospel (*The Rising Sun* and *Following Jesus*) are available on Kindle.

John and his wife Rosemary live in Pitlochry, Scotland, and can be contacted by email: jggreenshields@gmail.com

Nyomi Lee Purves lives in Fife, Scotland with her husband and baby daughter. Although working mainly in the care sector, she has developed and uses her artistic skills in her local church and community. Nyomi can be reached by email: nyomilee1994@hotmail.co.uk

Printed in Great Britain
by Amazon

24399892R00076